WOMEN AND SPORT

Spectator or player, amateur or professional — the pleasures and the pressures for every woman are examined in incisive style.

G000042200

WOMEN AND SPORT

FROM FITNESS FOR FUN TO
INTERNATIONAL COMPETITION
-THE PLEASURES AND PRESSURES
FOR WOMEN TODAY

LYN GUEST DE SWARTE

GRAPEVINE

First published 1988

© LYN GUEST DE SWARTE 1988
Photographs © EILEEN LANGSLEY 1988

British Library Cataloguing in Publication Data

de Swarte, Lyn Guest
  Women and sport.
  1. Sports for women
  I. Title
  796'.01'94   GV709

ISBN 0-7225-1374-7

Grapevine is an imprint of the Thorsons Publishing Group, Wellingborough, Northamptonshire, NN8 2RQ, England

Printed in Great Britain by Woolnough Bookbinding, Irthlingborough, Northamptonshire

10 9 8 7 6 5 4 3 2 1

Contents

Dedication

To Catherine Gibb with love, without whose selfless support this book would never have been written.

Foreword

Why do women compete in sports?—Why not!

For me the answer is simple. It is something I do well and that I thoroughly enjoy. There is nothing that equals the satisfaction and pride that is felt when I reach a goal. My goals are simple—to do my best and, by doing so, win a medal. Why a medal? Because it is a symbol of the recognition of my efforts.

It is a simple aim but for women especially it is one that is fraught with difficulties. For this reason I marvel at the number of women who actually make it to an Olympic Village. It is as if we are the tattered remnants of the Light Brigade, because, believe me, it has been an almost insurmountable struggle to get there! But we do it, and it is great, because it is what we want.

But it is not just olympic stars who enjoy sport—every woman should be allowed to discover exercise in all its forms, or be made aware of it, if they wish. You do not have to compete, but the enjoyment of 'playing,' which is what sport is really about, should not be denied to anyone.

This is what makes this such an important book. It is a concise enjoyable guide for *all* women interested in sport. It is written for all of us—from the mildly interested novice or concerned parent to the elite sportswoman whose aim is nothing less than international honour and acclaim.

There is a place for every woman in the world of sport. Read on and find yours—I hope it is as comfortable as mine.

Judy Simpson
Commonwealth Games gold medalist
1988

Introduction

Sports and physical play had no meaning for me until I was eight years old. Before this my excursions into the great outdoors were usually preceded by my mother picking me up kitten-style by the scruff of the neck, tearing me away from the handy corner into which I had tucked myself away warmly reading an encyclopaedia, and putting me down outside our kitchen door with the instruction to 'play' and 'get some fresh air for at least five minutes'. She would then bolt the door on my protest for the said amount of time. Like many other timid and studious children, I couldn't see the point in wasting time aimlessly playing, although I enjoyed the tap dancing and acrobatics lessons that were statutory for would-be film stars.

Then, one Saturday spring morning, I agreed to go to the local ice rink with my sister and the other children who lived in our road. I walked down the stairs inside the rink and I still remember that strange mixture of smells — of rubber matting, leather skating boots and mild sweat — that hung suspended in the freezing cold air. The shining white surface of the empty ice pad stretched out before me.

Trembling with fear and anticipation, I laced my feet into the hired skates and hung on like grim death to the three-foot-high barrier that surrounded the ice. The ice closed around the edges of the steel blades beneath my feet, and never let me go.

The 'tomboy' image

Happily for me, and seemingly unlike many of my sister sportswomen, I was never called a tomboy. This was possibly because of my previous preoccupation with books and the more gentle art of dance. According to the *Concise Oxford Dictionary*, New Edition, a tomboy is a 'wild romping girl who behaves like a boy'. This is social acclimatization with a vengeance. How much more easily girls and young women would slip into their chosen physical recreational activity and sport were this word and its archaic definition deleted from the dictionary and thereafter relegated to the scrap-heap.

In an in-depth survey carried out in 1979 by Glasgow University, 70 per cent of girls under the age of sixteen said that they found enjoyment in and satisfaction in sporting activities. The drop-out rate after sixteen and/or leaving school is horrifying. There is mounting evidence to suggest that a continuous mixed sports and games programme in schools could appreciably slow down and eventually, I would aver, halt this miserable trend.

One good thing about sport is that it teaches you to learn from those more practised and rehearsed than yourself — in this instance, the male sports *modus operandi*. How have they achieved their erstwhile supremacy?

To the victor the spoils

Male leaders have employed various strategies to ensure their continued control of the world's resources. In order to maintain their assumed domination, they had to devise a complex structure that would defeat the majority's understanding. The extent to which they succeeded can be measured by their manipulations of the world's population, using war tactics to decimate worrysome agitators, and instituting the divide-and-rule theory of the victor. To be victorious, you have to have the vanquished, of course, and what a good way to get your own way! War became the acceptable offshoot of territorial and proprietorial rights, and sport was then seen as acceptable combat.

When war was so carefully projected as a male practice, with its attendant glorified male macho image of the Hollywood movie — 'Heck, it was nothing', said with wry smile after wiping out the entire battalion of Japanese with one arm broken — is it any wonder that sport as 'non-fatal' battle also acquired a male bias?

There are several ways to perceive war, and subsequent battle positions, from a female stance. We can either view the women's sports position as one of being under seige, or we can view the situation as one of having been in the first place forced to retreat under fire. If we take the first battle position, then we have to lay up our supplies and wait with what would appear to be imbecilic hope for the gain of microcosmic concessions from the enemy without. Alternatively, and more effectively in my opinion, we can take the sensible overview and consider ourselves under attack. In this case, as in any honourable battle, the aim is to win rather than to go for a truce, and therefore the only reasonable plan is to reform and regroup behind our own lines. This, in fact, is our situation as it stands and having got off to what might be considered by our detractors — although not by our supporters — as rather a slow start, we are succeeding in gathering sufficient momentum to scale the heights we need to launch our onslaught. Ultimately, the aim is for girls and boys, young men and young women, old men and old women to come out to play in a spirit of mutual respect and co-operation, and to coexist peacefully on this planet. This in itself must be sufficient to rattle the creaking bones of the planet's ruling junta.

Society's role

It may well be that greater exposure and increased awareness of the mores of society at large plays more of a part in deterring adolescent women from physical activities, than any amount of rearrangement of body fat levels and other hormonal and biological manifestations chronicled so lovingly and in such detail by scientific and social diarists.

Like most women who have had the good fortune to be brought up in a pleasantly 'middle class' way in which they are cosseted until the middle teens, I had only experienced the fair play syndrome. It was not until I broke out of this comfortable way of life that I became aware of the discrimination that was subtly at work.

At the age of sixteen, my sport gave me not only a unique reason for living — but also a roistering social life centred around a clean and wholesome atmosphere. Unfortunately, for many young people, the ability to take part in such an invigorating pastime is dependent upon money. This factor is also a major consideration for women with children living on low or fixed incomes. There are some who consider youthful child-bearing in straitened circumstances reckless beyond belief or understanding. Nevertheless, it often happens. Whatever the reasons, there are plenty of women in this situation, and it is clear that we need many more concessionary facilities, including door-to-door chauffeused transport, to enable women with children to participate wholeheartedly in sport.

Women helping women

This problem is now in hand, in fact, with initiatives being taken by the few women who are actually managers in sports centres. Take the very good recognition of women's sporting needs by the London Borough of Brent council's Charteris sports centre in Kilburn. This is run by a woman who was also an executive committee member of the Women' Sports Foundation. The centre holds women-only sessions for all manner of sports and recreational activities, and actively encourages participation by what might be termed the most disadvantaged groups in our society, within those sessions.

The majority of coaches, administrators and recreation managers are men, so resource allocation, the development of strategies to improve and ease the entry to recreational and sporting pursuits by women, and any decision-making with regard to that within organized sports activity, can all suffer.

However, I still believe that each of us has a vast amount of determination and energy which can be brought to bear. Before women and girls can take advantage of any collective initiatives being taken on their behalf, they must call upon their own personal reserves of strength.

Women must be prepared to act on their own behalf in the fight for their social and sporting emancipation. We must be prepared to accept each other's differences, so that the disparate members of the women's team can score their single winning goal.

CHAPTER ONE
Fitness Boom?

Survival is one of the strongest of all animal instincts, and when a major part of that survival rests on physical prowess, the positive pursuits of physical fitness could be seen as a better class of primeval urge. The same could not be said for the close matching of protagonists in the confines of a roped off 20-foot-square area, beating hell out of each other and usually falling slightly short of murder.

The Aerobics Image

The male doctor, one Mr Cooper, who first isolated and identified aerobic exercise, was to women's sport and physical recreation what Rutherford was to science when he split the atom. Where the misuse of Einstein's discovery led to yet another inevitable war toy being produced, to the dismay of a greater part of the earth's population, both female and male, Cooper's effort was immediately put to misuse by that other faction without conscience, the commercial profiteers, to the great delight of that part of the world's population that demonstrates its mindless acceptance of many an establishmentarian plan, and agrees to exercise only within proscribed socially acceptable limitations. The mushrooming of aerobic dance-based exercise studios and classes had a double-edged effect. On the one side, women were demonstrating visibly their abilities to exert their bodies in a positive and recreational manner and not in the usual invisible domestic context — walking miles with a pram, or with heavy shopping bags, scrubbing kitchen floors, and often combining housewifery with equally taxing labour outside the home, or as most of us euphemistically call it, 'doing the double shift'. On the other side, the usual promotion of the singling out and separation of women from the mass, and the continuation of the projection of girls and women as rivals in some fantastic and nebulous competition — with an equally fantastic and nebulous male as the prize — shrouded the cause for equality in specific sporting areas in tailor-made obscurity. While those 'fitness' or 'aerobic' exercise classes organized by trained teachers at least imparted new levels of physical strength and self-confidence to hitherto recreationally inactive women, they were also recreating and reinforcing the socially stereotyped and male-defined standards of 'femininity'. For, while some women are happy to flash a pair of legs clad in green and white satin Lycra stripes and pink leg warmers thinking that men find this type of ensemble a turn-on, they are less happy to be seen in the more utility tracksuits and kits required for other types of sport, which they regard as a definite turn-off.

From a slightly different standpoint (and sporting activity), the comment of Cathy Mowat, Chairwoman of the Women's Cricket Association and Middlesex fast bowler, about the Indian women's cricket teams' sensible trousered kit, shows how confused the issue is at every level: 'We want to retain the feminine side of the game, and it could make it difficult to decipher whether they are male or female. There are various shapes and sizes in our teams, and therefore it's not conducive to the wearing of trousers.'

Whether or not we dress to please ourselves or our immediate relatives or to attract partners is undoubtedly up to us. Up to the present time, the only initiative ever taken on a large scale to dispense with that old and seemingly predominantly female worry about what to wear has been by the Chinese, and the only thing that they could come up with were old boiler suits — now to be seen in ever decreasing numbers on the streets of revolution.

However, in our freer market place, the law of supply and demand prevails and, following hot on the heels of the thousands of women shopping for aerobic exercise-insipired clothing, some far-sighted manufacturers of real sports clothes have started producing working tracksuits and running gear with 'gender appropriate' trimming.

Before my liberationist sisters interject, let me remind them that in the run-up to World War II, the idea of physically strong and 'naturally' beautiful women, clad in uniformly simple and puritan style was all part of Hitler's Volk Kultur. This, of course, increased the distance between those women who adopted that creed and the gypsy women and those whose more flamboyant personalities could not or would not be restrained in that way.

That women's spirit is indomitable is demonstrated by the fact that we have taken the good points from this captive situation — women are practised in making the best of a bad job. I have long held the view that the shiny skinsuits that belong to ice speed skating should be adopted for wear in other athletic exercise areas, particularly on the running track. Happily, a few athletes have been seen at public events wearing at least the bottom half of such suits. It was a crass piece of reactionary judgement that refused to allow a female tennis player wearing a white skinsuit to continue her game in the prestigious 1986 Wimbledon Championships. Unfortunately, the media seemingly decided that this garment had been worn, not as a functional piece of sports equipment, but as an alternative to a suspender belt and black stockings!

In fact, people wear skinsuits because they feel better in terms of freedom of movement. Body temperature remains normal for the task, with increased support for muscle. In an aerobic dance studio such a garment would have excited no more than a cursory glance, again reinforcing the concept of safety within socially agreed bounds.

Women have flocked in their droves to take part in physically strenuous extra-domestic activities in pursuit of muscle tone in the Joan Collins/Jane Fonda mould. Jane Fonda, having graduated through early pulp films to saving the world and Vietnam, took up the new aerobic fad with equal fervour and sold many tapes, records and books which assisted women to 'work out' without actually having to go out — another point in aerobic exercise's favour?

The glamour image has been promoted by the exposure of millions of women to the outrageous and decadent quasi-realistic lifestyles of Hollywood soap operas, probably embodied more by the 'well-preserved' appearance of the ageing Joan Collins than by any other member of the cast list.

How far have these image-makers departed from the tenet that you can't buy health or happiness?

Physical exercise is a wonderful thing if a woman in average health undertakes a fitness programme perhaps beginning with just five minutes in the morning and again in the evening. Increasing this energy output gradually over a period of several weeks, she will find an inner glow that will sustain her through some of life's most mundane or traumatic moments. If she then decides to put her new physical capacities to work for her in a more sociable capacity, she may find happiness in the companionship of a specific sports club, athletics club or communal sessions, either mixed or for women only, at her local sports or leisure centre. All of these activities can be geared to fit her pocket. In extremis, there is always the woman next door as a companion for a run round a local park, or even just round the block, on a regular basis.

The background to the boom

The idea of women's keep-fit took root in 1929 and, ever since women and children were brought up from the mines and off the fourteen-hour factory shift, there has been a slowly increasing awareness of the need to maintain this often homebound unpaid workforce in a reasonable state of health.

In Britain, in the pre-Welfare State era, most women, but particularly working-class women, were just glad to stay alive for as long as they could in whatever condition; for where life-expectancy for working-class males stood at thirty years in inner city areas before 1945, life-expectancy for females was generally more likely to be pegged at the birth of their first or subsequent children.

Any woman who has suffered the misery of anaemia due to pregnancy, dietary deficiency, or heavy menstruation, knows how debilitated that makes you feel — certainly not up to much by way of physical jerks!

Women's living standards improved with the inception of the National Health Service, better ante-natal care and better diet, together with anti-viral and anti-bacterial intervention. An increase in local government housing, complete with bathrooms, which dispensed with the need for the nail on the outside wall on which hung many a tin bath, improved the situation further, and it became more feasible for women to consider the quality of their life. Needless to say, an accompanying rise in wages and salaries then made women a prime target for domestic and beauty product advertising, blowing in on an ill wind from the United States of America.

Like a well-nourished child's first tottering footsteps that coincide with its growing awareness, these new, physically stronger women were finding their feet in what had hitherto been solely a man's world. In equally childlike frantic attempts to hold on to something they believed was theirs by right, and being far more practised and skilful in hanging on to territorial rights, the men found their stick to beat the women with — image and role. A lot of women themselves probably felt that, should they take on what was held up to them as a male role, they would become undesirable. And, should the whiteness of their washing let them down, they would be seen as uncaring — caring being the female watchword. Should they also be caught unmade up and unsmiling by friends, neighbours and, worst of all, their menfolk, this would be yet another nail in the coffin of their femininity and female usefulness. By the 'swinging sixties,' synthetic women were everywhere. The media-contrived images of feminity were copied by mini-skirted, high-heeled, bewigged, mascara'd women out on the town. At the same time, they wanted to be seen cosily settled in a gleaming kitchen smelling of beef stock cubes, caringly and smilingly looking after their model children, one boy and one girl. (The boy had to be born first in order to show the girl what to do!) By the 1970s, they were going to the doctors in droves for tranquillizers and anti-depressant drugs.

That same breeze that brought the advertising hit squads to Europe in the early 70s also brought the Women's Liberation Movement. After the first alarm, consumer interests rubbed their hands with glee. Here was the very happening they'd all been praying for. It was a man who first coined the phrase 'Divide and rule' and here in the 1970s millions of unsuspecting and unaware women were delivered into their hands. Wave after wave fell before the onslaught of male chauvinism. The popular press and independent television media controlled by their advertisers, churned out a barrage of acceptably feminine, youthful, chocolate-box pretty, sylph-like, submissively expressioned stereotyped role models. Patronizing male derogatory phrases, such as 'women's libber', 'butch', 'man hater', became common currency. As a last-ditch attempt to halt the advance of what Wilde prophetically called 'this monstrous regiment of women', we got the 'page three' pin-up.

The inevitable progression towards full emancipation by women was not to be stopped quite so easily, however. Some of us are made of sterner stuff. Sugar and spice is a pretty tangy combination.

The 1980s

By 1980, with a world-wide recession looming large on the horizon, sport — that hitherto predominantly male domain — was perceived by those who aspire to set the course of history, to be the haven (no doubt the assumption being at the time that this was to be for men only) of a new 'Leisured Class' — in other words, the soon to be millions of unemployed. This time around, the unemployed were not to consider themselves under-privileged and they were not going to loaf around on street corners looking miserable and hungry, nor were they going to betray the fact that they had a female dependent and/or children starving at home by selling matches with the usual placards. Instead, they were going to be part of a national movement towards a new technological utopia. They were going to be encouraged to spend their time in their local sports centre, kindly set up for them by a benevolent authority. These centres, of course, were to be managed and staffed by men. Sport was going to be the macho replacement for the male breadwinner's king of his castle image. At the same time, women were going to be able to keep up with the Mr Joneses by taking part in what was projected as a feminine recreational activity, where they would complement the male stereotyped masculine role by wearing pretty clothes sold to them in the High Street and, as they used to say in the East End of London, 'smiling the whilst'.

In 1980 at a holiday camp 'somewhere in England', for instance, a special session was held for women called 'Keep Trim with Tea', sponsored by the tea companies. This was carried out in 'aerobic' style, with a leader out front doing the simultaneous exercise demonstration. I don't suppose that any of those women knew how trim the women tea plantation workers were, from picking the stuff for hours in return for starvation wages.

This hourly work-out was probably the first ever organized aerobic dance class, and although the aerobics boom did not take place until 1983, this early manifestation was a clear indicator to those involved of the potential for exploitation.

Far from being a helpful and inspiring adjunct to the efforts of those women already engaged in pressuring the powers-that-be for more equality of opportunity in sport, the aerobic fad seems to remain an amorphous mass of perpetual motion. Marking time on its own spot.

Calling the tune

The idea of movement to music has always been an attractive one for human beings — especially, it seems, to women. Even this has been used against the furtherance of sporting equality. In gymnastics, the women's floor exercises are accompanied by music and marks are given subjectively for 'interpretation' incorporating the abstract 'feminine grace'. In order to raise the pulse rate of the aerobic exerciser, a variety of loud popular dance music is employed. While not in obvious open competition with each other, since pop music is mostly played and promoted by male musicians and singers, women are still dancing to a man's tune. I consider that the worrying amount of stress and strain injury finding its way to casualty departments and doctors' surgeries is the result of frenzied and frantic desires to keep up with the beat of the music at any cost. I began my involvement with dance at the age of four and gently grew with the art. I didn't have to dance the tarantella in my first lesson.

A champion sport fighter, Penny McGrory, says that her background of many years learning classical ballet, gave her the solid physical base for her prowess in her chosen sport.

While I am not suggesting that all dancers should become involved in other sporting pursuits, I am suggesting that many of those women who are involved in aerobics should contemplate putting their energy into sport or serious dance. There should be a concerted effort on the part of sports clubs, associations and organizations to recruit women from their aerobic classes. However, as most clubs, associations, organizations and sports centres are still male-run and seem content with the status quo, they may well resist this proposition.

CHAPTER TWO
Body Building and Weight Training

Because some members of my family were in show-business and because I showed every sign of wishing to enter that profession at an early age, I was privileged to watch 'artistic nude modelling' at a local Music Hall (long since demolished to make way for a shopping mall). The powers that be had issued an edict, in order to protect public morals, that nude bodies were not allowed to move on stage and this gave birth to the artistic static tableaux. These were a series of poses, preset either behind drawn curtains or on a blacked out stage, to be revealed fleetingly to the excitedly hushed audience. The models were mostly women, although there were scantily-clad speciality acts, predictably pairs of male and female body-builders who created sinewy and sensuous displays. I spent many happy hours backstage in the damp, raw brick dressing rooms made bright with dressing table lights and warm with the good humour and powdered bodies of the artistes.

Wishing to emulate these ideal women, and there not being any commonly available material on how to achieve this in the 1950s, I read the Charles Atlas dynamic tension method on how not to be a seven-stone weakling and get sand kicked in my face! The principles of his method, which could be practised in any spare bit of time in a minimum of space, have stayed with me until the present day.

Strong is beautiful

The pursuit of physical beauty above all else may be an unacceptably hedonistic concept within the term body building, and yet it is seemingly acceptable within the framework of the aerobic dance/exercise idea. Both set out ostensibly with the same aims, and yet are never parallel. The body builder herself is afflicted and is attacked by the self-same forces that extol the aerobic afficionado. The 'strong is beautiful' image that could be the very visible tip of women's strength through sport and recreational activity, is weakened in a welter of pouts and fluttering eyelashes that even the nude models in the music hall tableaux would have baulked at.

The Food Factors

As a sport, body-building requires as total a commitment as any other athletic pursuit to achievement of what is, after all, a very personal goal. Diet is a top priority for women wishing to build muscle. In this way, this sport could clearly show the way ahead to other sportswomen who very often perceive their dietary needs coming low down the scale of their training requirements. It would be interesting to make a large-scale survey of what our international sportswomen eat before going out and taking part in their particular events. I know of an international footballer who, having missed lunch, played a gruelling game on one chocolate bar without which, she said, she could not go on. Fortunately, the game was one-sided and her country won. During the memorable Indian woman's cricket tour, there was an uproar in the visitors' camp when they broke for lunch and sat down to light English luncheon of sandwiches, tea and cold drinks. They decided they wanted curry, without which they were not going to play in the afternoon. An alarmed English club official had to rush to the nearest Indian take-away and, although the Indian touring side complained afterwards that the curry was not hot enough, I shouldn't think that it did much for their game — they drew.

There must be many more instances of inappropriate food intake, and one could go on forever citing other equally telling examples.

Food for body builders is not just seen as fuel for energy output but in a total nutritional context and is designed to maximize the muscle growth potential and load-bearing capacity of the skeleton. In everyday terms, this means a combination of rigorous weight training techniques, either by the use of free weights or fixed variable resistance machines, and a low-fat diet. If you have to eat flesh, stick to boiled meat and poultry with the fat cut away (skin being the fattiest part of poultry), with a minimum intake of dairy products — and preferably none at all. There are now low-fat dairy products on the market, such as skimmed milk and low-fat cheeses.

It goes without saying that salad is good. All pulses and whole grains are great, and so are root vegetables. Body builders are also some of the most avid consumers of dietary, vitamin and mineral supplements. With the right training programme, overall strength increase can be 50 per cent after only a few months' work.

Carolyne Cheshire, Britain's top professional body builder, says: 'Body building and weight training are about knowing and becoming aware of your own body, realizing your own physical potential and not accepting physical limitations.'

Working with weights

I remember my amazement, when I travelled abroad to ice speed skating competitions in the early 1970s, on being told that the foreign opposition trained with weights. But in this sport, provided the skill factor is equal, the end result over distance is that the fittest — meaning the women with more cardiovascular and muscle strength — will win. I always lost.

Training with weights has improved British performances remarkably in the past few years. As weight training has become more and more popular, our achievements in track and field events and team games are proving that you can't keep a good woman down — access to facilities permitting.

The male regime may well have been thrown into confusion by the sudden and snowballing interest of many women who are breaking through the walls of their hermetically-sealed aerobic bubbles, realizing and identifying for themselves the need to create a visible muscle tone, the seeking of which will give them their ultimate freedom — whether they know it or not.

No discussion about weights would be complete without addressing ourselves to that most hallowed and ordinary 'truth' held so dear by reactionary employers in the early days of the 1973 sex equality bill. Advertisements for labour often carried the words 'some heavy lifting involved' or 'ability to carry heavy loads'. Any woman thick-skinned or silly enough to apply for these jobs would not be successful, all because of a myth masquerading as a fact — that women were too weak to carry things.

Those who would quote our biological and physiological differences in support of such spurious arguments should consider the load-bearing qualities of the female frame. In that most traditional capacity of child production, at the end of the forty-week gestation period, a woman has carried an extra weight of around 35 pounds. And she has never been able to put it down! If you have not experienced this for yourself, try hanging a large sack of potatoes round your neck at tummy height for a few hours!

A championship sport

Compare that attitude to the news that the first Women's Weight Lifting World Championships is to take place at the end of 1987. So far twelve countries are looking forward to this first truly international event, hosted by the USA.

Apart from the keen participation in America, the inevitable Eastern bloc contenders have been quick to sign in. In the last six years, many countries have instituted national championships, and under the leadership of Indira Ghandi, India, maybe surprisingly in the vanguard of reform, started a women's programme and produced extremely good results in their national women's programme and produced extremely good results in their national women's weight lifting championships.

Many women who have previously trained with weights for a specific sport are realizing their potential sporting achievement in what they had previously thought to be only a sport preparation.

Britain's Beryl Crockford, former women's world single sculls champion, retired from rowing last year to concentrate on weight lifting competition. At thirty-seven, she is still very much in contention for the British championship crown. The present champion is Diane Denham.

Diane gives the lie to the rumour that you need to be large and masculine to lift heavy loads. At 5 foot and 8 stone 2 lbs, she is the 52kg record holder in all three areas, the snatch and clean and jerk. She can snatch $57 \cdot 5$ and clean and jerk $72 \cdot 5$, making a total of 130. She is another woman who came in to competitive weight lifting by the back door of her local gym. As a keen winter sportswoman, she had wanted to improve her skiing performance and was shown how to improve her overall strength by using back squats and overhead squats. She found that she enjoyed the lifting for its own sake, and she also discovered women's competition. From then on, she went from strength to strength and in 1986 won the International 52kg class at the Pannonia Cup Tournament in Budapest, Hungary. Just to drive home the *real* truth about women's innate ability to lift weights to those Doubting Thomases, here are some repeatable words for their ears.

Everyone will agree that women have a greater flexibility and elegance of movement than men, and it's this that helps them in the technical performance of the movements required in weight-lifting, particularly in the classical heavy athletics exercises.

There are many other sports which, when analysed for their momentary strength resistance, come out with a far higher power strain than just the plain old 'ability to lift heavy weights' specified by the 'men only' job ads.

I always enjoyed acrobatics, and the feeling of muscle strength and control it gave me, and I was not really surprised to learn that when women perform a double back somersault, the power used is five to six times greater than their body-weight. For me, that would mean my weight of 7 stone 12 lb, which is 50kg, would multiply to a power of 250-300kg.

The heaviest weight so for has been lifted by an American woman, Karyn Tarter, in the clean and jerk of $137 \cdot 5$kg. The maximum power strain to her was approximately $226 \cdot 9$kg (this was in the $82 \cdot 5$kg category).

The shot putt is now a reasonably well-accepted discipline for women and actually generates more energy output and momentary strength resistance than lifting the heaviest weights. When the world record shot putt was set, $4 \cdot 8$ hp. was developed, whereas the biggest power developed by Karyn in the snatch of 105kg was about 3 hp.

Isn't it always the case in the fight for female equality that just as you think you've made up some ground — in this instance, argued ourselves into warehouse-type jobs — the requirements change! That same job ad would now read 'a degree in computer sciences necessary'.

CHAPTER THREE
Is Sport Fun?

For many years the only fun that adult women had from sport was the fun of making sandwiches, pouring tea, keeping score (for those of us who could count), washing dirty kit and generally experiencing the pleasure of cheering the men on.

For girls, there was the regimented fun of the school sports curricula with all the extra fun of stripping down to vests and knickers in chilly primary school halls. Even more fun was the scantily-clad PE drilling under the snickering gaze of youthful male classmates. Then, when you were old enough, you could have lots of fun trying to avoid the kind of games lessons of which the Spartans would have been proud. Of course, all this has changed nowadays. Fewer and fewer primary schoolgirls are to be seen cowering in a small corner of the playground while the boys occupy the rest of it with a full contact game of football. Instead, increasing numbers of schoolboys are confined to their corners while the girls play football, encouraged by a brave new breed of PE teachers. But this only happens in certain areas. At a crucial time for competition, when the old diehard tradition of a win at any cost is coming more and more into disrepute, of those who fail to support women's sport I would question their reasoning. Take, for example, the politicians who completely misconstrued a suggestion by the local education authority that where 'football was to be offered as an option for girls, netball should be equally an option for the boys'. They decided that this meant that if girls couldn't play football, boys would not be allowed to play football and would — horror of horrors — 'have to play netball'.

As men's football flounders in a welter of hooligan-induced electrified fences, photo pass cards and cross-Channel punch-ups, new games are being introduced to the British sporting scene. Games such as softball, korfball, volleyball and basketball, in which girls and women, as well as boys and men, can take part and excel, are becoming more popular. At the same time, as if by magic, and yet again from America, a new and even more macho, male-dominated sport — American football — is increasing its popularity by way of media attention. The fun that women can get from that is 'cheerleading.'

'Sport for All'?

Whether we take our cue from America or from Europe, the gains that women seek to make in the proper provision for their participation in any physical recreational or sporting activity, are proscribed and inhibited by prevailing socio-economic factors.

European political manipulation has had far more time to mature in subtlety than the more brash wheeling and dealing of the equally profit- and power-motivated United States of America. Great Britain, falling as it were between two stools, has always taken refuge in its own feudal system.

In 1966, the Council of Europe formulated a 'Sport for All' campaign, ostensibly to promote cultural development. In 1972 the British Sports Council was established as a direct result of the Council of Europe's recommendations. Ten years later, the Council of Europe established a permanent committee for the further development of sport and adopted a European 'Sport for All' charter. It recommended member governments to base their national policies on its eight principles.

Article I is that 'Every individual shall have the right to participate in sport'. Article II states that 'Sport shall be encouraged as an important factor in human development and appropriate support shall be made available out of public funds' — this last, an enjoinment to those communities most dedicated to 'free' and 'private' enterprise. They must have been expecting a lot of trouble. The Council focused European national attention on the spa-like, socially therapeutic properties of sport and it stated that the overall aim of its 'Sport for All' policy was to 'enable everyone of both sexes and in all age groups to preserve the physical and mental powers necessary to survival and to protect the human species from deterioration'! How does this sound ten years on, in the light of current common knowledge about the increasing pollution of our planet, due in no small part to increasing technological activity and corporate greed? It doesn't cost very much to extract lead from petrol and yet it is still belching out in many a European atmosphere. I wonder what sporting activity we could all take up to protect ourselves and our children from this kind of environmental brain damage!

Great Britain has managed to retain a greater part of its integrity by virtue of its historical hatred of its European neighbours. Britain mulled over the Council of Europe's recommendations and its principles, and exerting its expertise in sorting the wheat from the chaff of ideological invasion, it produced its own version of a sport for all policy to enable it to meet the needs of its indigenous island population. However, politicians, being what they are (and what they are is mostly male), have taken decisions on behalf of a preoccupied and recession-hit British public, that have propelled us towards a 'European' way of life and made it seem to our friends and allies who were previously part of the British Empire and now the Commonwealth, that they are out there on their own. Since when did the British ally with the Boers over their hateful white supremacist policies?

The unhappiness and dissatisfaction generated as a result of the British government not agreeing to apply sanctions against the apartheid regime of a former Commonwealth country, led to a boycott of the Commonwealth Games by many countries previously entered as competitors.

Britain with its traditions of free thought, illustrated by even its youngest citizens' obsession with free speech, and its generally unarmed police force, is a far cry from the more authoritarian regimes on the Continent. Therefore, it follows that British sports needs and requirements would reflect and resemble more closely those of its Commonwealth colleagues, particularly Canada and Australia.

In both these countries, new initiatives have been taken and, although 'revolutionary' in concept, they have been taken with the co-operation of their governments' sports advisory organizations.

Sports for women

In Britain on 19 October 1985, the Women's Sports Foundation was launched to promote the furtherance of equal opportunities and options for women in sport.

Although the real instigation was one of social urgency, it took female high-quality endeavour to form an idea generated by circumstance into a real and recognizable shape.

Women's harmonious enjoyment of sport is correspondingly diminished by the effort of finding a way in which to take part. Fun, this isn't.

For teenage women, access to socially acceptable sport and recreation is a fairly automatic process. There are many athletics clubs, often attached to local running tracks, sports clubs for girls who want to play tennis, table tennis, badminton, squash and so on and there is often little pressure on them, whether they wish to take part recreationally or compete at higher levels of competition, provided that they don't mind — or might welcome — the attentions of their male compeers.

Team sports are often a more attractive alternative for young women who prefer to be part of an organized group effort, and who have the desire to compete with them to a higher degree — team games are invariably about winning or losing — or for girls and young women who prefer the company of their own sex.

Even so, there are still prevailing economic and social factors which can filter through, even into the more rarified atmospheres of youthfully membershipped sporting enclaves.

While many over-sixteen-year-olds are able to continue their association with clubs and other focal points of physically recreational activity, those who have only enjoyed sport in their school environment are often lost. More recently there has been a phenomenal rise in participatory interest by young women in hitherto socially stereotyped 'male' sporting areas, such as rugby, soccer, cricket, basketball, mountaineering, outdoor pursuits and water sports. There has been an increasing demand for facilities to take part in snooker and darts, which up until now have been seeded and encouraged by way of the working men's clubs which have remained entrenched bastions of male chauvinism.

Winter sports facilities in Britain have always been extremely scarce and wherever opportunities for training are that thin on the ground, time for new women's sports activities is at a premium, if not non-existent.

The chance to compete

When I began my involvement with ice speed skating, there were fourteen ice rinks in the UK that afforded speed skating facilities on a club basis. Coupled with that was the fact that in 1973, to my knowledge, there were only three women engaged in the sport. Previously, Britain had had two speed skating women. One was Pat Tipper who set the British outdoor one-mile record for women in the 1968 Olympics and retired after marriage, and the other was Vicky Friend who set the British indoor quarter-mile record at 49·4 seconds on the old 125 metre track at Streatham Ice Rink on 8 November 1968.

I began training on a Wednesday night, at the unearthly hour of 11 o'clock, — a time to which I was going to grow well accustomed. Six weeks later, I was asked if I would like to go and race abroad with the club — this was the direct result of the refusal by Streatham's only competitive woman skater to go out, get seasick and get beaten. Where ignorance is bliss, wisdom is definitely gained at the expense of folly. I went. I got seasick. I got beaten.

I stood at the starting line with three Continental championship title holders, one of whom, not knowing my level of ability or lack of it, wasn't going to take any chances and, with what I considered to be the height of bad manners, kicked me as the starting gun fired. In what turned out to be one of the longest 500-metre races I ever entered, I had lots of time to ponder on the reasons for my imminent defeat. One very positive result of this disastrous first race was knowing that nothing could ever be that bad again, however far I lagged behind the winner in consecutive races, and that the reputation of the English for bravery remained untarnished. I was ever after referred to as the brave English woman who never gave up.

In conversation at the end of that first weekend's racing, Trudie Blumberger, Jackie Du Wein, and Sonia Candlebinder, my opposite numbers on the line, were amazed at the lack of training time I had had and the facilities I had been short of. They trained a minimum of three hours a day on the ice, six days a week, in an atmosphere of club and public support, where the men in their society found nothing strange in their desire to race on skates. Unlike at home, where comments at the time ranged from the 'serious' such as 'you won't be any good as a team member because you'll be ill every month', to the humorous 'the last time I saw a pair of legs like that, they were on my plate at Christmas', or the even more obvious 'you'll end up looking like one of those Russians' — and we all know what that means!

When I came home, I decided that my best bet was to encourage more girls to take up the sport I loved so much. The first woman to join me was the future bronze medallist in the 1978 World 500-metre Championships, Kay Dibbling — then an enthusiastic beginner in figure skating. We trained together and put on exhibition races at our home rink. This excited the interest of a woman who was training as a figure skater at Nottingham ice rink. Mandy Horsepool (now Worth), determined to beat both of us, hung up her figures, put on some speeds and began training with the men at her local club. She was soon followed by Kim Ferran from Solihull.

The first race in Britain, with its full complement of four women on the line, took place in 1974 at Streatham Ice Rink. Kay won, Mandy came second, I came third and Kim Ferran came fourth. All three went on to both set and break records, and to world class competition, and have helped by their example to recruit many more girls and women into sport.

The first British Women's Championship was held in 1981, and again the honour was given to my home rink by the Ice Speed Departmental Committee in recognition of the battle that had been won. I had lobbied for this event to take place for years, on the basis that unless women are given the same goals as men for which to strive, there is no purpose for them in a highly competitive sporting atmosphere and that recruiting girls and women was made that bit more difficult at club level.

Women in charge

In 1977, I retired from competition to coach and became the first ever female judge of ice speed skating. I was also nominated as my club's representative to the departmental committee that administered my sport within the aegis of the National Skating Association of Great Britain. In 1986, having served nine years as first 'B' class judge and then 'A' class judge, and having refereed the 1983 Easter weekend Youth International in Belgium at the same rink that had been the site of my first race, I was made the first ever woman full referee.

More and more women should not only be taking part in sport themselves and recruiting others, so that more and more women are able to share in their enjoyment, but they should also make every effort to enter and take part in the administration and coaching, and in the duties of that same sport.

The lack of womanpower in the organized sports hierarchies

has a direct bearing on the reluctance of girls and women to participate. Where the authority is male, it may be seen as at worst hostile and at best patronizingly over kind.

Executive women are most in evidence in the segregated single sex sports, although they certainly seem to flourish in much the same way as the Chinese Tongs, operating outside of the common public consciousness. It would be nice for these women's sports associations to seek a higher public profile. The only time that women's sports associations do get recognition is usually when they make controversial decisions regarding members with top-class sports reputations.

One such, much reported, decision was the Women's Cricket Association's dropping of pink-plaited Sarah Potter from an Australian cricket tour. More recently, the Women's Lacrosse Association saw fit to drop all three of its national coaches, the head of the three being the chair of the Women's Sports Foundation, Celia Brackenridge before even more mysteriously reinstating them.

In these instances justice 'seen to be done' can only damage the overall image of women's sport. Because most women who want to further the cause of women's sport know that the showbiz maxim 'no publicity is bad publicity' does not apply in our case, some highly controversial decisions, even when not taken in camera, are still seen to be, for the present at least, best left to fester quietly within our own body politic.

In newer sports, particularly those that until recently have only been played by men, problematic situations have arisen, caused by that single fact.

First on the post-National Health Service scene was women's football. In the wake of the Wembley World cup final in 1966 between our old foes the Germans and our own English team, the enthusiasm that was generated led to a new movement within the game's supporters. Hitherto having only seen themselves in servicing roles, reinforced by monstrous television adverts showing women washing their male offsprings' grimy football kit with brand X soap powder, women were awakening to the possibilities of kicking balls around themselves.

Coinciding with the Council of Europe's recommendations of their Sport For All policy, women's football teams began to emerge. By 1972, and again, as if by magic, coinciding with the new British Sports Council, women's football had established itself by the time-honoured custom of forming an Association. By this means the

WFA brought about the rescinding of the 1921 FA rule that banned women from playing organized football. The Men's Football Association still holds fast to its rule, even in 1987, that girls over the age of twelve are not allowed to play in mixed teams under FA auspices. One of the somewhat more imaginative results mooted by men, if this were to be allowed, is the vision of hundreds of boys, ostensibly not good enough for their first XI's, clamouring to be admitted to the girls' teams.

If we follow these various arguments, which in all cases seem to regard sportswomen as second-rate sportsmen, and the males attaching themselves to this second-rate manifestation as equally unworthy, perhaps those male managers and coaches of women's clubs and women's teams should bow out gracefully and let the women get on with it themselves.

Expertise is the direct result of adequate experience, and where the presence of men as mentors in hitherto male-designated sports activities may have been justified in the early days of women's football, since there are now over 200 women's football clubs affiliated to the WFA and twenty-three leagues in which they take part, there must be many women who could occupy those positions of power.

The battle to get established

It would be unfair to talk about women's ice hockey in exactly the same light as football, which is the British national winter sport. In Canada, where ice hockey is the national sport, women's teams have played as a matter of course. As an illustration of how hidebound British society is, women's ice hockey is having a very rough time indeed.

Male football is imbued with the need to prove that men's virility and warrior instincts are unassailably unaltered by our modern civilization. Ice hockey, with its larger-than-lifesize padded image, a game devised by intrepid adventuring men colonizing the wilds of North America, with women trailing along behind them, has been played like football on ice in this country. It has been promoted by ice rink managements, particularly those controlled by large business interests, who, watching the rise of media interest in all things macho and American, saw a way to improve their gate receipts through ice hockey.

Falling foul on all counts, the women ice hockey players have had to glean their practice time where they can, with matches fitted in and around heavily over subscribed male fixture lists, to the extent of only getting ice time in the leaner summer months.

Women from Britain were playing international matches as long ago as the 1930s and the 1940s, against teams with names like the Paris Belles. But with the wholesale departure from Britain of post-war Americans and Canadians, who were really the inspiration and driving force of the game in this country, general interest waned.

The men's game battled on with the help of the remaining North Americans until the late 1950s — with no women's teams to be found. There was, of course, the occasional pocket of resistance from their exclusion, such as the ill-fated attempts of some girls in London to hold together a team called the Harringey Rebels. Harringey ice rink shut soon afterwards and became a warehouse. They should consider erecting a blue plaque to my college friend, Marcelle Gibb (Mops) who would have been a really good goalkeeper.

In 1976, a young woman skater at Streatham ice rink approached me and asked if I would help to get ice time for a group of girls who wanted to play ice hockey. I tried but wasn't able to convince either my rink management or any other within a reasonable distance of the desirability of such a project. Still, my own sport gained several recruits and in 1978 Sue Parsons, Lynne Fowler, Lisa Jones, Bernie and Tricia Lacey and Anne Mear joined the Streatham ice racing club and trained alongside Kay Dibbling.

In 1980, Sue spoke to me again about possibilities of establishing an ice hockey team. We sent out letters to other ice rinks inviting replies from women who would like to play ice hockey. We hit paydirt. We were overwhelmed with the response. We once again approached the Streatham management and this time we got lucky. Yes, we could play an exhibition match and, yes, we could have a little bit of ice time to practise. We begged, borrowed, and some bought, equipment. One of the worst aspects of borrowing men's gear is lacing up shoulder pads and chest protectors, the bottom part of which only reaches halfway down over one's bosom — and then finding, as I did, that the end of a hockey stick can get jammed up inside the front of it. I played the rest of one game hoping that I was not permanently deformed. It wasn't until recently that breast plates became *de rigeur*.

That first game convinced our detractors that ice hockey was a women's game too. As a result of their speed skating training, the Streatham team forwards were so fast down the ice that goals were scored virtually before the other teams had moved after the face off whistle. What was lacking in stick skills and manoeuvrability was soon made up for by lots of very late-night practice, although for the many emergent club teams, such as the Brighton Amazons, it meant training in a local hall — no ice time!

The 'twelfth man' syndrome

In spite of these drawbacks, we established a Women's Ice Hockey Association. While it was accepted that only women would play in the teams, it was harder to hold on to the reins of womanpower in management structure. But men should not have control, however benignly administered, of specifically women's sports organizations and the only way in which control remains with women themselves is by constitutionally allowing men to be either associate members without a vote or co-opted committee members without a vote — this measure relegates male expertise to the advisory sidelines.

This may appear to be the simple solution we have all been waiting for, but reactionary social indoctrination, with its projection of submissiveness, helplessness and a necessary dollop of self-effacement as a goodly part of stereotyped femininity, makes some women and girls quite vocal in their support of voting rights for men, and all that that implies. These are the women who have acquired no armour for the fight. These are our friends and colleagues who are used to putting the needs of men before their own and who have been made to feel unsafe in the company of other women, some of whom may well appear to be stronger than they are and therefore, by association of ideas, threatening by the male definition of masculinity. The inference here is that women wishing to plot their own course are not behaving normally.

It has been my experience that these sportswomen are the same ones who do not object, in sports such as football and ice hockey, to the term 'ungentlemanly conduct', nor to the 'twelfth man' in women's cricket. In these contexts they are definitely not generic.

At one particularly tough ice hockey match, against the Peterborough Ravens at the East of England ice rink, Anne Mear, who had just punched somebody (by accident, of course), complained to me about the term 'ungentlemanly conduct'. The referee suggested that the booking be made for 'unladylike conduct'. I had a good laugh at this suggestion made in these circumstances. How about 'unsporting conduct' instead?

It's not much fun, either, having male coaches who are unskilled in female sports psychology expecting young women to respond to male engendered coaching techniques, especially of the 'those who don't complete this drill satisfactorily will do ten press ups' variety.

Unfortunately, even those women who have become extremely skilled in these so-called masculine sports still lack self-confidence, probably as the result of subjection to male authority and the opinion encapsulated within that, and so very few women proffer their services either as coaches or as top administrators.

And yet surely we can draw strength from those sports and recreational activities that have always been seen by both men and women as belonging to men alone and that are now being promoted for women as a result of initiatives taken by these same men. Here we see for ourselves the way in which women's sport can flourish when the men in that same sport do not feel foolishly threatened.

The English Olympic Wrestling Association instituted a programme for training women coaches to national level. There are competitions at all levels up to world championship class, for which preparation begins at local club level. The EOWA is so keen to help women wrestle and share in the enjoyment of the sport fully that they send female wrestling coaches to any group of would-be women wrestlers around the country at EOWA's expense. Although women's wrestling was not included at the 1986 Edinburgh Commonwealth Games, the EOWA appointed a woman sports doctor, Wendy Dodds, to their team.

A similar initiative has been taken by John Brotchie to enable women to learn the skills of sport fighting and to learn in such a way that they become proficient teachers themselves. (Sport fighting is a similar discipline to unarmed combat, much used by commando units. The object of sport fighting is to win by submission. Submissions are indicated by tapping the opposition on any handy part of their anatomy.)

The new 'leisure' age

For sport and recreational activity to be fun for women, we have to agree the concept that physically taxing effort is enjoyable for its own sake. Secondly, we must be prepared to find fun in the amazonian effort and energy output needed in hunting out and then making available to all women the places and the means by which they will so enjoy themselves.

Much of this work has been undertaken in the past within the socially acceptable framework of women's voluntary labour. By 1980, the more concrete results of European monetarism were beginning to manifest themselves in a previously dormant public at large. This contained the new 'leisured class', the part-timers, the job-sharers and the downright unemployed.

This last group are made to feel that their condition is all their fault, that they are 'spongers', and that they should be doing something about it. At the same time, the dawning of 'New Technology' produced the leisure age, with its accompanying 'let's find them all something to do' syndrome, is supposed to be welcomed in a big way. Given these conflicting attitudes handed out by the governing class, it isn't surprising that the enormous schemes launched by the Sports Council to encourage community sports and recreational participation have been met with some distrust.

Back in 1981 some of Britain's most disadvantaged citizens took their frustration and bitter anger onto the streets in some of the more run-down big city areas. After weekends of violence, the writing was on the wall and all right-minded people were agreeing that something should be done.

In the midst of all this toing and froing, the situation of women within this civic unrest assumed its historic role of invisibility. As a consequence, the Action Sport project, which was set up and funded by the Sports Council, did not make any original large provision for women, except under the heading of 'other target groups' and bracketed as usual with the disabled, ethnic minorities and those over fifty — which seems to infer that none of those sundry designations apply to women when seen as a group. This is no more apparent than within the designation 'unemployed', the common assumption seemingly being that the full-time 'employment' field is wholly occupied by women under twenty-one and men.

Many other initiatives were taken at this time by other organizations (like the Lords Taverners) and local authorities, but most of them suffered from the same lack of thorough planning in their haste to head us off at the pass.

The apparent main aim of the Action Sports project was to demonstrate the value of sports leadership in increasing participation in sport and recreation, but you can be sure that the benefit to the status quo in terms of return in public order for the expenditure of some £3 million by the Sports Council plus local authority financial input has been immeasurable.

Notwithstanding the male bias, women have been helped greatly by copycat community sport and recreation enterprises. Nearly all the original participating local authorities — six in the West Midlands and nine in London are now continuing the programme with 50 per cent funding from the Sports Council for the first twelve months in the West Midlands and for the first six months in London. Forty-five per cent of women who had not previously taken part in out of schools sports activities participated in the various programmes.

Overall, 13 per cent of people taking part were aged over forty, with the over sixties making up an enormous 65 per cent of this figure. Interestingly, twice as many women as men in the forty to sixty age group took part and four times as many of the over sixties. One of the reasons for this success is that those in the pensionable age group are often organized into clubs and have good social contact as a result. These are also the women in an age range that is most left alone by the advertising industry who presumably think that by the time we're over sixty, we've bought everything we're likely to want to buy and, with the wisdom acquired with age, we will not respond to distorted images of ourselves.

As women in the sixteen to twenty-four age range are the main consumer targets of the advertisers, carrying within their midst the casualties of a grisly media war, it's hardly surprising that as a group they were not keen on taking part. It would be patently unfair to put the onus of failure to take part on the individual lack of motivation in their besieged circumstances.

It's worth noting that, due to the same set of circumstances, women-only 'feminine appropriate' sessions, such as keep fit, had the greatest take-up of all.

The Women's Sports Foundation is the ideal link-up between women involved in both community-based recreational and sport programmes and the 150,000 voluntarily adminstered sports clubs in Great Britain. The WSF is the means by which the vast reservoirs of female knowledge in all sporting and physically recreational areas can be made to take visible shape.

At least there is the consolation that as time, and with it progress, marches inexorably on we shall have the fun of making sandwiches, pouring tea, keeping score, washing dirty kit and experiencing the intense pleasure of cheering *ourselves* on.

CHAPTER FOUR
The Competitive Urge

I can see no reason why competitive sport shouldn't be viewed as an enjoyable recreational pursuit. Arguments rage in the divided sports camp and, presuming that the anti-competitive faction would like to see the supporters of competitive sport back down, and if we take as a yardstick of competition the desire to beat the opposition, they have entered into a state of competition QED!

Instinct or enjoyment?

Competition is a natural phenomenon but should not be equated with the fascist evolutionary theory of survival of the fittest. Darwin's suggestion that we have involuntarily mutated in order to maximize our use of our natural environment is easily disproved. Any casual observer of the human condition can see that we are born very much at odds with it.

Our instinct to reach out for that which is beyond our grasp is just a basic requirement of average human development. The fun element in all this striving is often self-supplied in developing humans by instigating a competitive game to see who can get what they want first, whether or not anybody else has been made aware of the contest.

An even newer theory on our physical prowess, or lack of it, is that sufferers of back pain have inherited their symptoms as a direct result of our foremothers deciding to come down from the trees and walk on two legs instead of four. This theory takes no account of bad posture, beds that are too soft, many hours sitting hunched over work, having to pick up sundry small children twenty times a day or, given that there is no medical disorder, sheer lack of body tone.

Unlike us, the animal world has not been gifted with reason and they are not able to organize their instincts as we are for our greater enjoyment. Their competition is usually a near life or death situation, often in terms of who gets to mate with whom. Our version of competition takes place on a far higher plane, although the former makes the underlying motivation behind sports like boxing and full contact American Football easier to understand.

Is it an accident that rugby players or wrestlers have the appearance of rutting stags, and could this be the reason for all those men-only sports being defended so furiously? Is the new women's emancipation in sport, with its attendant role reversal, part of the inevitable evolutionary process or is it revolutionary?

I'd say, lets go for the revolution. Female rivalry remains a fermented source of profit for men, who control the great majority of the world's money, and misery for women, who don't. Competition between women is a far healthier manifestation when it occurs in a controlled setting, in exactly the same way that the sports field or boxing ring has expurgated the rivalry between men. Women bring their humane qualities with them into the fight. The basis for fair play, is an honourable contest.

Honour is a built-in part of the female psyche, and the Japanese male searching for his honour, and exalting it beyond all reason, could be the victim of vagina envy. Japanese paternalism is being challenged in a simple and direct way, even if unknowingly, by women who have taken up judo. The Japanese have, nevertheless, introduced such aspects of their chauvinistic culture as the mindless tea-break factory work-outs to Great Britain. Physical exertion should not be compulsory; better the availability of facilities within the work environment for both men and women to enjoy a lunch-hour work-out in a gym or a knock about with a ball.

Winning at all costs

However high the level of competition, most women would agree that the concept of winning at all costs is the worst precept in the world. Success is a far more subtle expression and contains a finer definition of the quality of effort involved.

In the 1980 Winter Olympics, during the ice speed skating heats, one of our women, Kim Ferran, was racing neck and neck, when the other woman fell. Kim stopped to help her and lost that chance of winning and with it a medal. There should be other medals struck, for those more abstract triumphs.

The greatest satisfaction of all is for an individual to know that without a doubt she has done her best. One of the nicest things about my own sport is that the effort made, from the fastest to the slowest, the oldest to the youngest, is always noted. In ice speed skating, at least, we don't suffer from that awful syndrome, those nameless also-rans — or rather also-skateds.

Taking part in a competition with the sole object of winning leaves no room for qualification in human terms. Taken to its extreme, it can actually make a mockery of itself without any prompting. Even at as high a level as the Olympic boxing tournament, a boxer can win by a walk-over if the other combatant fails to appear.

Sport is riddled with argument about competition and its consequences by those who disregard all the other manifestations of competition in other areas of human endeavour. If those who so frequently vocalize their desire to abolish competition — or any striving in a competitive manner generally — succeeded, what an outcry there would be from promoters of excellence in the arts.

One of the oldest musical competitions in the British Isles is the Eistedfodd in Wales. Singing is not a spectator sport in Wales, where the majority are participators. The culmination of the annual Welsh singing competition is when the audience rises to its feet and sings its response to the winner. Consider how fraught the perilous journey was in the light of all that audience expertise. The kudos that attaches itself to the great international instrument-playing competitions is not gained by wallowing in recreational musical accomplishment, pleasant though that may be. By the same token, that recognition of application which results in an Olympic gold medal has little to do with recreational sport.

For the disciple of dramatic art, competition stalks the most domestic village hall audition, and plays as much havoc with the nerves of West End chorus-line hopefuls as with those of England netball squad women waiting for the team to be announced.

Competition — East v West

Competition is an integral part of human dynamics and neither capitalism nor socialism can make it their sole prerogative. Those upholders of socialist principles, who are the main detractors of competition for its own sake in Britain, are lucky that sport isn't the religion of the socialist Eastern bloc countries, including the Soviet Union or they might well find themselves excommunicated.

The USA, their capitalist cohorts, and more especially the Japanese, have elevated competition to the level of human sacrifice on the altar of private enterprise. The revolting over-commercialized circus called the Los Angeles Olympics, now thankfully fading into the mists of time, did not prove that competition is a bad thing, only that it is vulnerable.

The socialist bloc, in the true spirit of competition, immediately staged the 'Friendly Games'. But, as there is not a statutory impartial panel of judges, coupled with the fact that the duration of the contest has not been fixed, the question of whether there will be an overall winner or whether the outcome will be a draw, and what the prevailing socio-economic factors shall be at such a time are yet to be determined. One thing is certain, however, if we all sit back helplessly, it is going to be determined without us.

On the move

Our contribution in sport to the principle of competition is ultimately the effort made to resolve the difference between what we want to achieve and what our physical limitations are.

I belong to that category of simple sport with the most obvious aims. I am proud to be labelled Transport. The criteria for using any kind of human transport is firstly will you or your message get there safely, and secondly, how soon. Translated on to a track or course (as in cross-country or downhill skiing, running, eventing and so on) you soon find yourself competing with the clock. The need to get from one place to another quickly and safely has been with the human race since the beginning of time. Apparently, even our modern Olympics stemmed from that ancient Greek message runner.

Competition in the transport sports is against the clock first and any other individual second. Unless, of course, you're an indoor short track speed skater, and under the conditions of contest there are four heats in which the first person in each heat goes through, plus a fastest second, and you have the misfortune to be behind a slower winner.

People have often asked me what pleasure I get from skating round and round in circles. Well, skating in a straight line has a lot of physical pleasure attached to it, it's the nearest thing to flying that I can imagine. But skating in circles has a spiritual continuum. From the whirling dervishes in the East to our own witches in the West, moving round in a circle in anti-clockwise direction is the key to the universe and the meaning of life. Modern civilization has carved up time into the manageable proportions of a mathematical formula, but it still refuses to work in a straight line. One of the most addictive properties of track racing is that the devotee is able to alter her perception and that of the onlooker of the passage of life time. In this way, human beings can at least temporarily gain an ascendancy over their fate. A race must start at a time of zero and from then on until it ends, that time is taken out of its ordinary context and becomes more akin to suspended animation. All forms of organized sport have pre-designated time formats: football with its forty-five minutes each way, ice hockey with its three twenty-minute periods and lacrosse with four periods of twenty minutes each are good examples.

They are good examples, too, of the fact that time itself can be used as an instrument of power. The old excuses for not allotting sufficient time for women's sports must be challenged. Why do women ice hockey players play five minutes less than men every period, and why do they often not get an overtime period? Why, even in international competition, do women footballers only receive forty minutes for each side of the game and, much worse, why is women's lacrosse allowed fifty minutes only with a maximum ten-minute half-time interval?

Other segregated team sports have similar time discrepancies and these must be resolved. The Marquis of Queensbury himself would have had to agree under his own rules of fair play.

With women's fitness levels increasing rapidly, male-dominated sports organizations must not be allowed to use the so-called weakness of our fair sex to demote women's full participation in such sports, particularly on the outmoded basis of inability to keep up the pace!

Eventually, even in these team sports, the two opposing sides are ultimately fighting the inevitable referee's whistle which signals the end of the time allowed for their game. How many last minute heroic dashes have been made down the mid-field or centre ice to score that vital goal in the face of the inexorable tick of the count-down stop watch?

Competition equals aggression?

There are those who advocate the abolition of the competitive concept, who argue that competition is bracketed with 'male' aggression in sport and that this juxtaposition militates against a majority female participation.

This is a classic media-induced hallucination — the majority of real-life men involved in competitive sport do not recognize or welcome the media male stereotype presentation of themselves. There are always exceptions to any rule, but when we are dealing with generalization, the majority disposition alone is worth considering.

In my own sport of ice speed skating, men and women compete together in a spirit of mutual enjoyment and co-operation, as they do in korfball. Korfball was created in 1902 by a Dutch schoolteacher, Nico Broekhuysen, who understood that competition can encompass the principles of equality of the sexes, equality of responsibility for decision-making and can be non-aggressive in the sense of physical contact.

To emphasize how mixed competitive sport can be made fair and possible, we can again look at Nico's method. One of the most obvious physiological differences between men and women is average height. In order to obviate any physically-induced discrepancy in performance, the height of the net or korf (basket) was set on a 3.5-metre (11 foot 6 inch) post, high enough to make skill alone the deciding factor.

One of the most common complaints from women and girls who play team games such as hockey with males, is that in commonly-found situations where the boys are more practised and possibly fitter and faster — however temporarily — they can easily exclude girls from the game by not passing to them. This situation can be easily remedied, providing that the organizer of such a game takes some time out to expound the principles of fair play and the benefits of not patronizing one's opponent, either in terms of allowing them to take the ball or puck or make the run or pass, or by whitewashing them.

Competition, not compromise

Competition is part of our lives. Both individually and collectively, none of us would get anywhere without a competitive spirit. One of the most defeatist sentences a woman was ever made to say in public is also, unfortunately, one of the most famous. The antithesis of women's liberation and all that we can gain for

ourselves through sport was the line in the film *Now Voyager* back
in 1942: 'Why reach for the stars when we have the moon?'

CHAPTER FIVE

Who's Media Is It Anyway?

Question: 'What do you feel about your treatment by the 'gentlemen of the press?'

'Diverse in a word. In some respects, they have been most generous and treat you as firstly, an athlete and secondly, a woman. On the other hand, they treat you like a sex object, certainly in my earlier years. I found I was taken lightly as a passing fancy, when I should have been earning respect. I am sure that men don't have to go through the same sort of apprenticeship as women do.'

So says Beryl Crockford former Olympic Rower and World Champion Lightweight sculls.

Alternatively, here's the view of Sarah Potter, Britain's top woman cricketer. 'Well, I think there's been a mixed reaction. Obviously it's a disappointment that women's sport in general, never mind women's cricket, is not represented fully, but having said that, I do actually appreciate why that is so. Women's sport does tend to be much more of a minority sport than men's sport, but on press reporting, you can't expect much more than you get.'

If the population of the West had remained largely illiterate, and had Lord Shaftesbury and Lincoln never been born (or at least been born without a social conscience), had Baird and Edison failed in their attempts to present flickeringly life-like images to an admiring audience, and Marconi failed to transmit ethereal speech, those with less than philanthropic motives who build public buildings, including sporting centres and venues, we would still have to rely on stained glass picture windows for the purpose of consumer brainwashing.

Before the majority of people were able to communicate by means of a rehearsed written language and when this important medium was used for the obvious sole benefit of the church and ruling classes, the only way of presenting the case for the acceptance of their lot was to surround the populace in their religious assembly halls, with graphic details defining sin and the wages thereof.

Women did not figure largely in these depictions unless as providers of apples or as vestal virgins and mostly foolish ones at that. Neither has this male-defined image of femaleness altered much over the centuries. If anything, with the increase of literal and visual sophistication it has worsened with its evolution.

The old adage of male appeasement, it has to get worse before it gets better, is small consolation for those of us who are suffering this minute.

The image of women

In a modern world where women are still viewed as as much of a marketable commodity as any cow, camel or performing seal, it's hardly surprising that what they actually say or do is deemed unworthy of remark or record. References to the female of the species are invariably couched in physical terminology, in much the same way that one might read, hear or view reports from a cattle market. Unfortunately, just as our senses can become anaesthetized by constant assault, so our sensitivity to the reception of inappropriate description becomes dulled.

Blonde curvacious mother of three; wife of him; forty-year-old; tall; elegant; short; plump; cuddly; cute; blue-eyed; quiet; sensual; long-legged; brave; courageous; one-legged; attractive; girlfriend of him; looking for the right man; home-loving with her companion of many years; promiscuous; pregnant; not pregnant; divorced; soon to be married; not interested in settling down yet; witch; he says she's a bitch; a good laugh say her friends; swam the channel/flew the alps single handed; won the marathon yesterday, and still looked good afterwards. . . .

Sunday supplements often excel in converting facts to fancy, as in this report on windsurfer, Clare Seeger: '21 year old blonde', or 'with a strength that belies her delicate features', 'while not forgetting numerous domestic duels with men.' Here Clare is reported as saying: 'We may not be so strong and fearless but we can make our sport look a lot more graceful and attractive.' The writer adds 'Clare you can say that again'!

Another discusses Jarmila Kratochvilova, the ex-World Champion Czech distance runner. 'This mature woman' and 'Kratochvilova cuddles a small girl who comes over for her autograph. Her mood drifts from motherly to girlish.'. . . 'One benefit of sharing her homeward journey is to study through the driver's mirror the blue grey eyes, the fine eyelashes she still guards from a visitor's direct gaze.'

Even a 'quality' paper like *The Observer* produces the ages of sportswomen litany as if to ward off some unspecific evil onslaught. 'Attractive 17-year-old. . . 14-year-old. . . schoolgirl — 18-year-old. . . . . . 40 years younger. . . at the age of 65.'

During a West Indies versus England men's World Cup Series one day match in Brisbane, Australia, the commentator, Desmond Lynam, remarked: 'There are other good things around to look at as well as the cricket.' The camera had zoomed on to a woman in the crowd wearing a brief summer frock. Would he have said the same had it been a women's cricket match?

And even the 'liberal' *Guardian* worries away at the heels of our progress, albeit more invisibly than it's blatantly bigoted Fleet Street and Wapping tabloid stable companions. In a seemingly pro women's sexual equality article, it nevertheless belittles Lorna Vincent, a professional jockey of ten years standing, after her win at Ascot thus: 'Lorna, *an attractive brown-eyed brunette, is still only 27* [my italics], but after an initial blaze of success her career is barely aglow now and she is in no doubt why that should be. Mention sexual equality to her and she falls about laughing'. . . Don't we all.

Added to this we see the transference of the male sport as war tradition, masquerading as news.

'Kitted out like a contingent of Ronald Reagan's Star Warriors, a team of Canadian women ice hockey players will do battle with a home-grown hit-squad who rejoice in the name of Streatham Strikers.' Had I known five years ago when we took a vote in the Streatham women's ice hockey club changing room on the suggested names for our team which all of us had put forward, I would have pushed harder for my choice, 'Streatham Rebels'. I wonder what the weavers of tales could have conjured up from that. All I can tell you is that the Canadians who had come over here to play a round of non-physical contact friendly games were outraged at this report.

The invisible sportswoman

Then what of our present-day glass pictures? It's easier to draw conclusions about motive, in the context of commercial television, for the preoccupation of its sports editors with male sporting and megabucks inspiring spectacle. It's a much more subtle exercise when it comes to the output from the British Broadcasting Corporation. It must be safe to assume that part of the beebs responsibility is to a bureaucratic male-dominated establishment. How else can we interpret the ludicrously minute percentages of screen time devoted to women's sport.

On 15 December 1985, they produced a ninety-five-minute review of the year's sport and they allotted a princely 3 minutes 49 seconds to women. The tally for the same programme at the end of 1986 was about the same, give or take a few seconds. Alison Fisher, the snooker champion, was pictured holding a bunch of flowers for three such ticks with Zola Budd claiming 18 seconds worth. Women won 30 world titles in that year.

Had they tuned into a splendidly entitled programme *Fifty Years of Sport: A Two Hour Sport Extravaganza* any visiting Martian might have been forgiven for assuming that there had been only half a dozen sportswomen of note during the aforementioned time span, and that organized sport and sporting events for women did not exist. That this was a true reflection of BBC outside broadcast coverage of women's sport could not be denied. Even on the 'alternative' channel, men's basketball is played to the dubious accompaniment of scantily-satin-clad females dancing around on the sidelines to taped pop music. This does not bode well for future serious coverage of women's basketball games. Furthermore, this kind of media acceptance of, at worst ignorant and at best naïve expression of support for sport does nothing to enhance its own image or to increase the numbers of women basketball players, now standing at the 4,000 mark. On the plus side, at least both the cheerleaders and sports participants were in an equal state of undress. Keeping in mind the relationship in our civilized society between clothes and power, particularly socially constructed quasi-sexual situations where fully dressed males accompany, or are in close proximity to, semi-clothed, although acceptably dressed females, the role of cheerleaders at other male sports events such as American football, are made even more doubtful as to the kind of support the men are being offered.

As Chair of a local association, I heard a suggestion that young women figure skaters should provide a squad of pom-pom waving cheerleaders for the local men's ice ball team. Having made a fairly reasoned and calm protest, I was told that this was show biz and what good fun this was going to be. No doubt we shall see more of these enthusiastic young women on yet another minority sport programme.

There is no justification for the media exclusion of the many and varied women's sports that take place throughout Britain on a daily basis.

Women who take themselves seriously enough to pay annual membership subscriptions to sports' governing bodies are numbered in millions. The Women's Squash Rackets Association enjoys the allegiance of around 25,000, the All England Netball Association are still top of the women's sports league with the paid affiliation of around 40,000 players. Compare this with the men's Football Association's register of less than one quarter of this number on their books. There are 22,000 senior female hockey players in England alone, with 500,000 — yes half a million — younger women registered enthusiasts in schools. The Women's Cricket Association can boast of a player membership of several thousand and the Women's Lacrosse Association who are commonly considered to have an even more rarefied membership roll, supports the participation of 40,000 players. They are hoping to increase this number, with the advent of a modern game called 'pop lacrosse.'

The assumption has always been that women, given the opportunity to take part, consider physical recreation and sporting activities as a waste of their time. This time being much more valuably spent looking after everybody else and ensuring that the interests of sportsmen and boys are caringly served.

No need at this time to elaborate on our common lot, the washing of male kit, the serving of refreshment in male sporting preserves etc; although I would like to think that this detailed explanation will be necessary for the informational benefit of future emancipated generations.

A negative picture

The negative way in which women's sport is depicted by the majority of media outlets does not happen in isolation, and when it is added to the equally negative media portrayal of women even in the most traditional of roles, it produces a positive contempt.

In a world hitherto controlled by men, as apprentices we should look to the jockeys and trainers in our search for comparable expertise. If the leaders of men are made on the playing fields of Eton (and all other predominantly male sports training camps), the leaders of women should and will come from those areas set apart for female sports participation.

While boys' schools such as Eton, Harrow, Winchester and Rugby and their state-run emulators are held in awe and respect by media presenters et al, natural enclaves for the pursuit of youthful sporting achievement which we call girls' schools have been the butt of many a derogatory comment by film makers, stand-up comics, the popular press and television commentators.

The most famous image is that of 'St Trinians', projected on film as the archetypal model for all girls' schools. The staff are portrayed as eccentric, isolated and frustrated women. Their pupils as either emotionally retarded nineteen-year-olds bursting out of undersized school uniforms, or extremely plain pre-adolescent twelve-year-olds for whom games were an opportunity to beat up the opposition.

It isn't hard to make the connection and association of ideas between that and the BBC Radio II sports presenters' attitude when previewing the England v Canada women's hockey international game on 15 March 1986 at Wembley: 'By the way, with thousands of screaming schoolgirls going to the hockey match at Wembley this Saturday, there will be traffic chaos in town.'

Or how about *The Daily Mail*'s contribution on Tuesday, 25 November 1986: 'And their netball has more in common with John McEnroe's tennis than a St Trinians off-season friendly. These girls are athletes.' Millions of us who have played off-season friendlies would take issue with the inference that it is a non athletic pursuit. This writer by his own bias, is assuming a separation between netball players that cannot actually exist. It also does a disservice to all those who are trying to encourage the sport at school level in order to ensure future world class participant competitors. 'Eighteen highly trained young women slugging it out in pleated mini skirts . . .' Presumably, if this kind of reportage fires some media marketing man's jaded appetites, we can all look forward to greater exposure of the game. Oh yes, I forgot to mention the sub-title of that piece: 'Netball's warriors follow hockey into the limelight'.

With the present controversy raging around the issue of competitive sport within school curricula, it ill-behoves sports journalists to knock any kind of school sports rooted activities-particularly those within the designation of team games. Of course each and every sporting activity has its exponents, who would loudly proclaim that their particular exercise was the best, whether it be within the rather more communally-inspired group effort or the more insular individual solo performance.

All of these human disciplines are worth reporting for their own sake, without unnecessary and inappropriate terms of reference.

The publicity dilemma

As far as the recipients of media 'with strings attached' attention often welcome publicity for their sport, they are equally often outraged by it. Netball, for instance, now enjoying a newly sponsored public enthusiasm, is also facing all the engineered presentation and misquotation previously enjoyed by men's football, cricket and snooker. Neville Southall, Everton's goalkeeper, was driven to wearing a tee-shirt printed with the legend 'I Love My Wife' after media conjecture about his extra-marital activities; we need no explanation of the refreshments of Ian Botham; and the public discussion of Alex 'Hurricane' Higgins' lifestyle — these are all examples of the exposure which, for men, has been a matter of course. Heather Crouch, the England women's netball coach is in the rather more privileged position of being given a right to reply here.

Heather was reported as having read a good luck card before the Australia v England game at Gateshead in November 1986 which, according to this particular reporter, '. . . seemed to sum up the new thrusting face of netball'. The card read "all the best girls and I think the phrase is — screw the b . . . . s"'. Heather afterwards described how the reporter pushed them with leading comments and questions to provide his readers with what he thought they might expect to find interesting reading. She felt that he was looking for an angle and, not finding one, used the ploy of getting Heather to repeat out loud this card as if she would have done this in the normal course of pre-match events. 'I guess he did it knowing that it was a one-off article — if he comes near us again we'll lynch him.'

Eschewing violence as a recreational pursuit, whether organized or spontaneous, we can all nevertheless make the necessary distinction between the orchestrated reading of a violent message, and the response of a victim to an aggressor.

One of the paramount qualities of sportspersonship has always been restraint from a position of strength. Penny McGrory, the British Sportfighting Champion who could lay out any of her opponents — male or female — anytime she felt like it, certainly possesses it to a much greater degree than the Solihull Vixens ice hockey team forward, who body checked Canada's Super Veteran, Mabel Boyd, breaking the game's code of non-contact and with it the guarantee of her own safety on the ice!

Most games and sporting pursuits constrain their participants within clearly defined rules. It is, seemingly, the infringements of these rules of fair play that excite media interest. Were Penny to actually harm an opponent, not only would this be deemed newsworthy by those who control the news, but her sport would suddenly evoke media interest where there has previously been none. Women's ice hockey, on the other hand, is gradually 'enjoying' more publicity with every penalty. As yet, neither of these two sports have attracted sponsorship, in common with many others.

Commercial sponsorship

Britain's Women's European and World Champion javelin thrower, Fatima Whitbread, is not a man — if she were she would still be sponsored by the West German company Adidas. Adidas marketing executives may well be causing their firm to under-realize their profit potential in the light of an increasing participation rate by women in sport — after all, every sportswoman needs a tracksuit. How is this happening?

After Fatima was dropped, the daily paper *The Independent* reported that Adidas executive Robin Money said in explanation: 'It's a male-orientated market that we are in and men have more influence on the consumer.'

When sponsors *are* found, they can often have an adverse affect through the ignorance and preconceived notions of marketing and business procedures on the part of the administrative officials in the chosen sports.

The sponsor takes on the mantle that had previously been worn only by Santa Claus. If any sport had an uncertain social cachet before sponsorship, you can be sure it will take a dive afterwards in its bid for the very popularity which will, the administrators hope, attract more lovely sponsorship money. Unfortunately the sponsors' priority is company name exposure and air time. The press are notoriously reticent to fill their column inches with the names of these modern-day philanthropists and, although producers of televised sports don't have to edit in quite such an obvious way, they can still pan away from the perimeter hoardings, and they very rarely zoom onto the score board, where it is often made apparent that a particular company is the 'best'.

Newspapers, magazines, other periodicals and independent commercial broadcasters are all shored up by their advertisers and, as yet, although we have advertising features contributed by companies in the world of paper and ink, audio-visual sponsored programmes are not seen or heard in our living rooms.

With the advent of cable and satellite television, a possibility would be to use sponsorship money in the production of a half-hour programme of women's sport interest and have it slotted in. This could well be something like 'Highlights from the Women's Football Association Cup Final, commentary by Rachel Heyhoe Flint, brought to you by Mrs Bakewell's Traditional Barley Water'.

Sponsorship of sport is now running at around £120,000,000 a year by commercial companies, in contrast with direct government aid through the Department of the Environment of around £30,000,000. Even so we'll probably have a long wait before one of our native sponsors can compete with the Antwerp Diamond Cup Association who donated a 700,000 dollar diamond-studded racket as a trophy for the European Champions Championship held annually in Antwerp.

Sponsorship is usually seen as an assistance to the governing bodies of sport and, in the promotion of their events, it is usually offered in terms of clothing, sports equipment, subsistance money and the occasional car to sportswomen already enjoying a fair amount of media limelight. Large capital investment such as training centres for athletes or training rinks for ice skaters is not forthcoming, although this would appear to be a very good way for the donating company's name to be enshrined in bricks and mortar for posterity. Because they forgot to put their name up over the entrance, how many people realise that the tobacco company WH & HG Wills built and sponsored Hickstead — the mecca of equestrianism?

Vivien Saunders, one of Britain's best-known professional women golfers and a former British Open Golf Champion, decided after applying for twenty-six jobs as a professional at various golf clubs that the chances of obtaining such a job were remote. Instead she spent the last few years combining writing about golf and coaching many of Britain's top women players with her job as a lawyer.

On the 24 November 1986, Vivien bought a golf club near St Neots in Cambridgeshire, which she intends to develop as a national golf training centre. A clear case of 'if you can't beat them join them and then beat them', and if you are able to take the risk then sponsor yourself, and others.

One major item of expenditure for Vivien will be hidden from public gaze, but will be constantly scrutinized by her accountant: tax. This only proves that Governments know a good thing when they see one and, with the coupling of commercial enlightened self-interest with the not-so-enlightened self-interest of most sports personnel generally, Government is able to avoid taking any initiative in the matter of sport providers' tax relief and exemptions.

Sponsors, after all, are seeking through their public choice of sport to promote a wholesome and healthy image for their product, not to mention vital statistics for their sales graphs. They are not likely to spend too much energy on seeking tax relief on their donations, an activity which might be seen as revolutionary in some quarters, but may be prepared to look for tax relief by creative accounting in their annual profit and loss figures. Sports people, on the other hand, particularly those who are singled out for sponsorship by dint of their single-minded devotion to their own achievements, are not renowned for rocking either their own or other people's boats.

By comparison, both sponsors of the arts and the recipient artistes and artists are usually the most vocal politically. It's therefore not surprising to find that they do enjoy beneficial tax reliefs. The one way in which sport could involve itself in seeking the change in this law, without having to appear too radical would be to call for fair play, pure and simple.

Bearing in mind that sport generates more money in commercial terms than the Arts (for instance, in television revenue), the Government makes its money twice. Once by taking tax from all quarters, and twice by making a saving from inadequate capital and revenue expenditure provision. Because central British Government will not spend sufficient money on sports development and promotion projects, the possibility of this ever becoming a major political lobby area is increasingly remote — and thus leads inexorably to the consolidation of capitalist enterprise in the form of sponsorship company associations.

The Sports Council itself has introduced its sports sponsorship advisory service which, in conjunction with the Central Council For Physical Recreation, performs the role of a broker — bringing business and sports interests together, ostensibly for their mutual financial advantage accompanied by prestige and popularity. This is not just a static professional advice-giving office — the service actively seeks out large companies who have not yet made their mark in this area of the sports world and tries to interest them. Sound advice is given on packaging and costing to governing bodies of sport and the SAS maintains and promotes contact between outside sponsorship consultants, public relations companies and promotional agencies. Constantly updated information is put out on a regular basis to all interested parties by way of a bulletin.

From inaugeration in 1982 to 1984, a very short time indeed, it generated sponsorship totalling £750,000, which helped sports as diverse as table tennis and ice hockey. This service should also take on board the issues affecting women and sport, and develop a method of transmitting examples of good policy and practice to those personnel involved in promoting their company's corporate image.

Until now, sponsorship services operating outside of Government remit have rarely manifested an awareness of these issues, even as a minimal requirement of their project. The Women's Sports Foundation have prepared an awareness training course in conjunction with the National Coaching Foundation and the Sports Council, which we hope will remedy this prevailing lack of insight and give another positive dimension to commercial interests.

Media portraits

The other side of this coin is that, in presenting this absolutely unique and first class awareness package to consumer oriented companies, we are disobeying the first rule of poker — 'never show your hand'. No one could dispute the fact that the Advertising Standards Authority have been made very well aware of the many and varied ways in which the advertising industry attacks women, by a constant barrage of complaints about the worst excesses of the commercial images of women throughout the whole spectrum of the media; and that equally there has been a refusal to uphold any but one or two such complaints over the last eighteen months. What we have seen is an even more subtle approach in those areas which give rise to most informed concern.

It isn't good enough to say that women are not for the most part concerned about pornographic depictions of themselves — that women and young girls may turn away from anything that makes them feel uncomfortable, threatened, or 'funny' to use the child abuse psychologists approach when warning youngsters about those who might physically invade their sexual privacy.

We are going to have to ensure that it is not just the advertising media that sit up and take note of this free market research, and that we should take every step possible in order to reach the women for whose benefit the work has been undertaken.

The knowledge of our sometimes Pavlovian predispositions is a priceless piece of artillery in the targeting of women as a consumer group — although sportswomen as a group have not suffered any more as a result of discriminatory advertising than their less active sisters.

There is a hunters stealth about the way women are customarily portrayed, which works against the interests of women who are sports enthusiasts. Women without muscle, who are weak-looking and immaculately done up all the time are an even less realistic mirror image to offer sportswomen although, perversely, to the point of insult, they are often graphically associated with sport for men. Many a sports equipment manufacturer (and sunbeds spring to mind most readily) offer such images as their sales pitch, and it's about time that self-respecting sportsmen, who themselves are being hunted by the same wolf pack, double back and defend their own integrity as well as ours.

A women's 'general interest' magazine, operating within the establishment definition of what we're interested in, asked if they could attend an ice hockey training session with a view to taking photographs. *Not* to encourage any positive thinking on the part of their readers, *but* as part of a 'before and after' advertorial. The club was asked to provide six blondes (I was asked but declined . . .!) without any make up on. They would be snapped, wrecked after training, and thereafter whisked off — a suitable verb without a doubt — to a beauty parlour and smart shops and photographed again. Fortunately, for unknown reasons, the project was dropped after the training session!

The media is extremely adept, or so they would have us believe, at giving the public what it wants. An 'us and them' situation if ever there was one. Who says we want to spend Sunday watching over-sentimental old movies full of outdated reactionary ideas, instead of the Indian women's cricket tour or the Great Britain v France women's rugby match — and why do 'They' think that 'we' wouldn't swop our expensive brand ABC 1 soap powder for the differently packaged but otherwise identical cheaper soap powder Brand X? This unfair situation has arisen just because of the involvement of vast multinational companies with the media and the way in which they are able to control the output.

Sport has long been regarded as character-building, and it was an American judge who said that 'we don't need that kind of character in our girls.' Obviously, he was only echoing the thoughts of millions of his compeers. The kind of thoughts that are grist to the free world's media mill.

The communication and information system which is termed 'the Media' has become a puppet without obvious strings, and one who's nose does not get noticably longer as it tells lies. It maintains its self-projected bland image in a way that is reminiscent of Oscar Wilde's *Portrait of Dorian Gray*. Although Oscar Wilde was not alluding to our subject, nevertheless I'm sure that he would agree, having been villified by the press in his own time, that we might make this comparison from his tale about a good-looking young man obsessed with maintaining his youthful outward appearance, who keeps a portrait of himself locked away which takes the brunt of his debauched lifestyle over the years, while he apparently remains unblemished.

That we actually have to buy into communication and information facilities is as outrageous in concept as having to pay someone else for our lives. Even more outlandishly, we are made to pay for what is mostly distorted, biased information and un-representational reflections of our own and others' daily lives.

The only way in which sportswomen will get the public recognition they deserve, will be if a Ministry for the Media is set up by the Government, which will work within the framework of this country's principles of democracy, and with a national network of media Enterprise Boards to encourage participation at grassroots or paving-stone level. This will ensure that every section of the community is represented on local press and broadcasting boards, and that includes sportswomen.

CHAPTER SIX

Dying to Win

In the old days, Eastern Bloc women were often kicked out of competitions when their male hormone tests proved positive — I think it's safe to assume that these were the first imbibers of the now-popular anabolic steroids, and not actually the men in drag that the sports authorities would have had us believe! I hope the Press sisters, at least, are now living in luxurious recompense after their guinea-pig-style exits from international sport.

To talk in terms of gaining an unfair advantage over the next competitor is valid as far as those who do not take the stuff are concerned. It is equally so for those of us with an overview of the debilitating long-term effect for both user and for sport as pure human physical expression. However, for those sports people, particularly sportswomen, who are caught in the maelstrom of a generally drug-tolerant, over-ambitious and critical society, the argument that drug-taking is cheating may seem very weak indeed.

There are far more insidious ways of damaging our health than smoking cigarettes — but it's a handy way of focusing attention on one dodgy item while the rest are allowed to whittle away undeterred.

Those who use drugs which they know to be harmful are the victims of the distorted values of the society in which we live, and in their behaviour society's attitude to sport is reflected.

'Social' drug-taking is often associated with problems of personal identity, an inherent lack of self-esteem and a consequent lack of confidence.

One major plus for sport and recreational activity is that it can offer a reasonably uncomplicated relationship with other people, can improve someone's feelings of self-worth with the acquiring of specific skills, and consequently gives a measure of self-confidence to even the shyest participant. To close down the 'natural high' which sport offers by polluting it with drug-induced euphoria is unforgivable.

If sport, as controlled physical effort in a recreational or competitive context, can be promoted and preserved as an honest and health-giving pursuit, it will be harder to justify its corruption by those who see sport as a profit-making exercise.

Early revelations

In the late 1950s American universities and high schools employed coaches for sports. They were usually employed on a one-year contract. If the students they coached were successful, they were re-employed and if they produced an unsuccessful team or athlete, they were sacked. What better method to keep one's job than to feed the competitors for whose results you are personally responsible performance-enhancing drugs?

In 1970, there was an inquiry by Congress on drug abuse in sport, and many American Olympic gold medallists admitted using drugs.

Although there was increasing disquiet about the use of drugs, there was a feeling of helplessness within the international governing bodies. There had been an unofficial testing at the Christchurch Commonwealth Games in 1974, but no action was taken against the nine sportspeople who had been found positive. The first real effort was made in 1976, when there was drug testing during the Montreal Olympic Games. There were many disqualifications of weight lifters and, in the women's discus, one woman finalist was found to be positive and was then disqualified.

It was an ill wind that blew nobody any good in Europe, West or East. At the 1978 European Athletics Championships in Prague, nine gold medal and world record holders were found drugs positive. At this time, there was no test for excess testosterone, although the medicos were analysing for steroids, steroid groups and stimulants — the assumption being that steroids would be used by athletes who needed to maximize their power over a short space of time as in sprint and throwing events. When three women middle-distance runners, who were among the best in the world, were disqualified after being found steroid positive, it soon became obvious that this illicit use of hormones had other effects. Unfortunately, it was discovered that an athlete could take them in training for an annual international competition for ten of the twelve months prior to the day, discontinue them for two months but still retain 90 per cent of the questionable and short-term benefit, and the steroids would go undetected at the event, at least by chemical analysis. Used during a training programme, steroids improve recovery rate — which is considered to be the measure of physical fitness. As a measure of real physical fitness in terms of the whole person, and life expectancy, this is laughable.

The earlier tests at top-level competition were concerned with defining the sex of the competitor. After puberty, the male body starts to produce large amounts of the masculinizing hormone testosterone, which causes muscles to become larger and stronger, while the female body produces large amounts of the hormone oestrogen, resulting in feminine fat. While much is made of the equation of pure muscle with strength in sport, female fat is a critical endurance factor, meant to take us safely through the labour of childbirth, but equally able to take us on a 3000-metre skate, a twenty-six-mile run, or a twenty-one-mile swim.

Types of test

'Sex' tests were introduced in the early 1960s to prevent *men* from competing as women, a situation which was quite prevalent up until that time. We will never know whether the Polish sprinter, Ewa Klobukowska, who failed her sex test in 1967, was another steroid job or was really a man!

Sex testing is a very simple process. Some cells are scraped from the inside lining of the cheek and are tested for Barr bodies. The number of Barr bodies in a cell is usually one less than the number of X chromosomes carried. Average men who have only one X chromosome usually have no Barr bodies. Women who have two X chromosomes usually have one Barr body in each cell.

An even simpler and cheaper test would be to pull their pants down to see what equipment they have, as they do in the army. Alternatively, they could count their ribs — men have one less than women. A more expensive way would be an X-ray photograph (observing the fourteen-day rule) or an ultra-sound scan of the pelvic regions.

After the new gender-determining test, when men could no longer be passed off as women, athletic and team coaches sought ways in which women could be made much stronger, or masculinized in terms of musculature.

In much the same way as the splitting of the atom was prostituted, the discovery of synthetic anabolic steroids by Dr Charles Kockakian, of Alabama University, before World War II has been misused. The same steroids that are given to prevent protein loss in very old patients and were given to concentration camp survivors to help rebuild their protein stores, are being used in the pursuit of self-satisfaction and greed.

There has not been the same emphasis on screening for adverse anabolic steroid group effects on women as there has been on men, but we can make some assumptions nevertheless.

Side-effects

Anabolic steroids can help in the treatment of osteoporosis, a condition of calcium loss from bone which begins in women at around twenty years of age, and increases gradually until it becomes more marked after the menopause (unhappily, the first real sign of this condition is often the breaking of a bone more easily — as in a fall without undue force).

Because men naturally have thicker bone, the immediate effects in bone thickening may be masked, although their sperm production will be reduced and testicles shrink (another obvious point in the 'cheaper' test).

For women, the results may be less acceptable — the hair on the head will thin in a male pattern of baldness. The hair may grow back after they have stopped taking the steroids, but the newly abundant facial and body hair will not fall out. This male hormone will also make a woman infertile, at least temporarily, and although fertility may be restored on cessation, there is no evidence as yet from which to draw a conclusion.

Women suffering from common gynaecological ailments such as endometriosis are treated with anabolic steroids, and the majority of therapeutic drugs used in the treatment for conditions in women caused by hormone dysfunction, will show up as positive in routine screening tests.

Women competitors will have to choose between finding acceptable alternative treatments or opting out altogether and take up coaching and administrating instead.

Just like every other chemical therapeutic agent, anabolic steroids have their side-effects. There is proof of liver damage and liver cancer, with an increased risk of heart attack or stroke. The risk of acne and a deeper voice may pale into insignificance before these greater dangers.

Synthetic growth hormone, too, is now being abused. When the only source of growth hormone was from the pituitary glands of dead humans, it was in short supply and was usually reserved for children whose stature as adults would be stunted.

Today it is being ingested, again as a size and strength intensifier, by would-be world champions, and seekers after temporary and temporal fame and fortune. Growth hormone raises the blood sugar level in the bloodstream and could result in diabetes — it can also lead to mineral retention, and too much of these deposits can disrupt ordinary bodily functions.

As with any bone-thickening hormone, facial features will coarsen — can you imagine a female Desperate Dan look-alike contest? This should be the only competition open to those who wilfully misuse this drug.

Women competitors who risk their well-being and physical appearance in such a devious manner will harm and ultimately kill far more than themselves — they will bury sport for all women and girls if they become the only role models available. It's hard enough as it is to interest and keep young women in sporting activities without the added deterrent of having to look like King Kong as a prerequisite of success.

The use of growth hormone is going to be the most difficult to detect in tests, and therefore to stamp out. It is absorbed so rapidly by the body that is undetectable within a very few minutes of taking it.

Stimulants

With all the controversy raging around hormone consumption, one might have overlooked the stimulants which are now back in the public eye after startling revelations in the Press about snooker players!

In 400 B.C., competitors were drinking a potion made up of ground horses' hooves boiled in oil and garnished with rose petals, to give them a boost. More recently, they have been risking cardiac arrest with amphetamines, caffeine and cocaine.

These are the drugs that affect the central nervous system by causing adrenalin production, which prepares your body for action and produces the 'fight or flight' syndrome.

In order to help you act quickly, the blood supply to some parts of your body actually shuts down. The blood vessels of the stomach, kidneys and intestines contract. More blood needs to go to your brain, heart, muscles and skin, and therefore these blood vessels expand.

These are possibly the most dangerous of all drugs to abuse, particularly as they are highly addictive and this kind of drug abuse overlaps into other areas of life. These are the drugs that cause hyperactive physical behaviour, accompanied by overactive, irrational mental processes, and bring into the hopeful field of sport and recreational activity the stench and despair of the gutter.

Apologists for the use of narcotics in sport will point to their 'plant' origins and to the ancient and primitive cultures who use them for what they would promote as beneficial effect.

Ginseng is another much vaunted 'natural' giver of safe extra strength — but its chemical component, damatrene-triol-glycosides, works like caffeine and only produces more adrenalin. Who needs more of that in a competitive situation? I used to feel sick and shaky enough before big events — extra adrenalin would have brought me to the point of collapse, as it would anyone else.

Muscles use both fat and sugar for energy, and muscle fatigue occurs when your sugar supply runs out. The role of adrenalin is to cause fat to leave the fat cells within the muscle and pass into the blood stream, which causes muscles to burn more fat and less sugar. This in turn gives you more time and effort before muscle fatigue sets in. The payback of misusing adrenalin-stimulating drugs is physical exhaustion, long-term mental psychosis and panic attacks. All these are associated with drug-withdrawal symptoms.

Painkillers

The other misuse of therapeutic medicine is when it is involved in shutting off the awareness of pain caused by physical effort. I've seen a few women taking aspirin-based products before training sessions and races, in an attempt to stave off the point at which they would otherwise be forced to stop. This is the stage often called 'the wall', through which one either goes head down or gives up in the natural course of events. On the other hand, if aspirin is taken to mask the pain of training or competing with an injury, and if this allows you to continue to overuse an already damaged part of your body, you could end up retiring sooner than you expected.

Aspirin — although it has been proved to have bad side-effects, such as dehydration by increasing urination and perspiration plus the risk of a reduced red and white blood cell count, possible stomach ulcers and asthma, is now being overtaken in adverse effects by the newest international pain blocker from the United States which is now in circulation — Dimethyl Sulfoxide, or DMSO. This is a by-product of the paper industry. It is highly carcinogenic, with the short-term effect of stopping pain in the same way as a local anaesthetic without the numbness. It is administered by placing it on the skin. It then passes through the skin layers into the fat underneath and, from the blood vessels in that fat, it then circulates through the bloodstream to your muscles. In animal tests, eye damage has been reported, as has liver damage in humans.

Legal relaxants

The last set of abused therapeutic drugs I shall mention are the Beta Blockers. These are used wholesale by archers, pistol shooters, and parachutists to reduce their blood-pressure and therefore their heart rate, and to relax their involuntary muscles.

In a competitive situation, anxiety and anticipation cause a natural surge of adrenalin and noradrenalin. Noradrenalin acts on Alpha responders and adrenalin on Beta responders.

The Alpha-type within the sympathetic nervous system cause the blood vessels to constrict in skeletal muscles and the Beta system stimulates the heart but relaxes the involuntary muscles.

Beta Blockers prevent the body's responses to the Beta influence of adrenalin, slowing the heart rate and steadying shaky hands.

Many years ago a male champion in pistol-shooting competitions put his success down to being able to control his own body responses from within. It was a much talked-about feat of human triumph over physical limitation.

This, surely, is part and parcel of sporting skill and discipline. What justification can there be for putting a score total before pride and dignity. If participants in sports such as the modern pentathlon produce certificates to say that team members suffer from high blood-pressure — and many countries competing at the Los Angeles Olympics had such certificates — should they not be competing alongside our registered disabled brothers and sisters? These were athletes who could race 4000 metres across rough country, and it would seem in fact that their medical stories were fiction.

Beta Blockers belong to those sufferers who truly need this drug to help them enjoy a reasonable physical existence. People who do not need them to pace an irregular heartbeat, to reduce muscular tremor or for angina — and make base use of them for their own satisfaction — are just plain cheats.

An illegal relaxant

Like pistol shooting, there are some sports that have identified specific problem areas for themselves. One of the strangest — and one in which few women take part at present — is speedway racing. There is a problem here with cannabis (chemical constituent Tetrahydrocannabinol, THC) and the organizers of speedway racing want to make it a proscribed drug.

The reason that non-motorized sporting disciplines do not seem to have a problem with this particular drug is that it actually has a notably *bad* effect on those wishing to physically exert themselves in exercise.

Only one cigarette containing an amount of cannabis leaf does the damage of sixteen ordinary cigarettes. The massive inhalation that is the trade mark of the dope smoker keeps smoke in the lungs for a longer period of time then the average 'pull' on a cigarette. This is because it takes longer to release THC from the carbon particles in the smoke to which it attaches itself than it does to release nicotine.

Tests have shown that after smoking only one cigarette containing cannabis, heart rate increases 34 per cent at rest, 18 per cent during exercise and a whacking great 50 per cent during the recovery period. Instant unfitness.

This increase in heart rate is caused by nerve stimulation alone. It does not, therefore, cause the heart to beat more forcefully and consequently pump more oxygenated blood to the muscle. It just works harder to pump the same amount of blood as before, making the body more tired while it feels 'relaxed'. This effect could be gained simply by exercising in the first place!

The danger to motorized sport is that cannabis impairs judgement and reason in a similar way to the action of alcohol. No one should be in charge of a piece of moving machinery when they are patently not in full control of their faculties. Cannabis and alcohol may not kill the drivers but they could certainly kill and injure others on the track or circuit with them.

Of course, as with every other sport, women are becoming interested and taking up motorized pastimes — let's hope that they don't involve themselves in the darker aspects.

Defeating drug abuse

Great Britain has taken much of the initiative over drug control, both in its methods of implementation, such as sampling and testing procedures, and by attempting to persuade sporting organizations in every country to hand out deterrent suspensions to athletes violating the rules.

This still is not enough to wipe out drug misuse altogether, because of the complexities of the problem, but it must help.

It may well be that Britain's simplistic solutions to crises are the best, given the overwhelming social and political nature of this terrible situation for sport.

This is a clear case for those umbrella women's sports federations worldwide to link up and stop the rot. We should all as women be committed to the improvement of the quality of life and not lend ourselves to its destruction, either by design or by default.

One of the major problems in the control of worldwide drug abuse is the varying restrictions on supply. Anabolic steroids, for instance, are freely available for sale over the counter without prescription in many Continental countries, which makes export and import on the black market a simple business.

The more the drug abuse problem escalates, the more hopeless will seem the task of eliminating it. We must all support the work being done by the British Sports Council in setting up models and giving funds to various sports organizations within its cadre.

In 1978, a drug control centre was set up at Chelsea College, London, supported by the Sports Council. It is one of the few laboratories accredited by the International Olympic Committee's Medical Commission.

Urine sampling is the most common method of testing because it can be collected by medically unqualified personnel, and it is also more likely to contain higher concentrations of drugs than a blood sample.

Unfortunately, this can cause great embarrassment to female participants because the surveillance woman is often known to them, especially in smaller sports like my own. Some of the girls who were tested at the British Ice Speed Skating Championships, held at the East of England Ice Rink in Peterborough, told me that they found it virtually impossible to pass any water because their embarrassment caused their muscles to contract. Nevertheless, we must all do our best to close our eyes and think of England — or Britain — in support of testing as a deterrent!

Random selection is made, usually by a committee set up for that purpose by that sport's governing body. As an example, they could decide before an event that the people to be tested would be the person placed third in the first heat, the person placed second in the second heat, and those placed fourth in the third heat, and second and fifth in the final. This method is scrupulously fair as no one has prior knowledge of what these placings will be.

As soon as the specified event is over, the selected competitor is notified, given a drug control test form for which her signature of acknowledgement is obtained and she is then asked to attend the drug control station.

Her time of arrival at the station is noted on a sample collection control form. There is a special directive that under no circumstances should members of the Press be allowed to be present.

The competitor is then asked whether she has taken any drugs within the last forty-eight hours. It has to be made clear that 'a drug' can mean any substance taken into the body which is not a food, including vitamins, aspirins and oral contraceptives. Details will then be noted on the form. Soft drinks are normally available to help promote a water supply. The competitor is then accompanied to the toilet by the appointed steward.

The toilet must be checked beforehand to ensure that no urine samples have been left there previously. The competitor then has to be observed discreetly to ensure she does not dilute her sample with water from the closet. One hundred millilitres of urine should then be divided into two containers, previously chosen by the competitor on arrival at the station. One container will be used for the first analysis and the second is used as a reserve sample should it be required. These sample containers are then sealed in front of the participant. They are coded and the code numbers are then entered on the sample collection control form. The competitor is then asked to sign a confirmation that she is satisfied with all the details of the collection procedure. Any objections are noted in a remarks section, before she signs. The sampling officer countersigns the form and, when all the samples have been collected from the event, they are placed in two outer containers. Each outer container is sealed securely, chilled or frozen and despatched to the lab as soon as possible.

There are obvious difficulties in collecting and monitoring out-of-competition samples. Drug control stations could quite easily be set up at squad training sessions, but the problem is that, in a country where sport and recreational activity is still highly disorganized, even many top-level competitors do their own training. It then becomes a matter of would-be competitors allowing a medical officer or someone so designated by that person's sport controlling body to collect a sample by visiting her at home.

Once a testing system has been set up, what is to happen if a lab finds traces of a banned drug? The Chelsea College has suggested a possible procedure. The lab should inform the sport via the official who requested the test. The competitor should then be informed and told by her governing body that she may present her case, and that she may also request that the second reserve sample be analysed while she and a representative are present.

After the second analysis has been performed and the report sent to the sport, the governing body can then consider the case and impose any appropriate penalty.

However abhorrent some of us may find the thought of 'catching' possibly misguided and weak rather than evil sports people, we must still consider the necessity to restore an overall opportunity for a beneficial lifestyle in an increasingly seamy, greed-motivated and lazy world.

CHAPTER SEVEN

Minority Groups — Minority Rights?

Having embarked on my chosen sport at an early age, it wasn't until I'd passed my fourteenth birthday that my father, coming to collect me at the ice rink one Sunday morning, inadvertently noticed me skating, only because he had arrived a few minutes earlier than usual. He beckoned me to him with an imperious gesture and, after two quick circuits of the rink, I sailed to a spectacular hockey stop in front of him.

I was greeted with 'Is this what I've paid out all this money for, for all these years, to watch you going round and round like a goldfish in a bowl? I thought you'd be another Sonja Henie by now!' He then muttered that he would wait for me outside, and that was the last time he ever saw me skate.

I fared better with my mother. She came to watch me for the first time when I was in training at the same rink sixteen years later. She sat at the rink side in virtually the same spot where my father had stood all those years before, looking conscientiously interested but slightly chilled. She then accompanied me to an international race meeting at Brugges in Belgium a few weeks later.

In 1981, when I was forty my mother again visited the ice rink to watch me coaching her grandson, who was about to be placed third in the first ever junior British Ice Speed Skating Championships. It was her turn to call me over from the centre of the ice, where I had been timing my son. 'I've got to go now dear, but I must say that I think you are being a little too hard on Leigh. I just thought I'd tell you how I felt.' That was the first and last time she ever watched him skate.

Why all this disinterest in my sporting activities? Having been born into a Jewish family, I was not expected to interest myself in anything as philistine as sport. Within the context of Jewish tradition, I did not suffer discouragement because of my gender but rather because of ethnic aestheticism — nobody ever watched my brother on school sports days either!

Apart from obvious hard and fast religious orthodoxy, which would certainly militate against women's participation in sport, plus a general restriction on anything but prescribed activity on the Sabbath, which stretches from sunset on Friday 'til sunset on Saturday, there are parallel philosophies which makes it de trop to take part in anything which might smack of human animality. Because, over the centuries, people living beyond the pale of Jewish existence have perceived Jews as a non-physical group, it has reinforced modern-day concepts of Jews having brains and no brawn. They have also mistaken dignity for cowardice and reluctance for inability. The inauguration of the state of Israel in 1948 went a great way towards altering some of the most common misconceptions about Jews with reference to sport in particular.

Suddenly there came the opportunity to take part as an identifiable nation occupying its own piece of ground in world affairs. This was a country not only peopled by survivors of death camps where many had filed with quiet dignity for their turn in the gas chambers, rather than sink to the bestial level of their captors by trying to kill them instead, but also with people who had fought back and survived barely armed rebellions, such as the Warsaw ghetto uprising, and fought against both the British and Arab armed forces.

Death at the Olympics

Outside of Israel there have been many instances which record negative feelings towards the Jews as a group. Very few non-Jews have taken up cudgels in defence of any other identifiable minority or oppressed racial group. This has also served to convince Jews that sport, with its avowed ethos of fair play, providing 'Leaders of Men' may not actually mean them, or extend to Jews generally. One of the most shocking and shameful examples of the kind of negligence to which I refer took place at the Munich venue of the 1976 Olympic Games. Eight Palestinian Liberation Organization terrorists invaded the Israeli quarters in the Olympic village. They took nine Jewish competitors hostage, with two of their coaches. Lord Killanin, then President of the Internationl Olympic committee arrived back for an emergency excutive meeting from Kiel where he was going to watch the yachting in the company of the head of Krupps, in a Krupps private plane. For those who might not know, after World War II, on hearing evidence that Krupps used slave labour from the concentration camps, and that some of these Jewish slaves were hanged with piano wire in full view of their fellow workers as an object lesson in productivity, the Allies promised to shut them down.

The terrorists demanded the release of 256 Palestinian prisoners held in Israel in return for the release of the hostages — Israel refused to trade and requested the postponement of the Games. They were postponed, but only from 3.30 p.m. until the following day. Meanwhile the German government had moved marksmen to the site. At this point, the terrorists were threatening to bring out and shoot one hostage every hour. Just after midnight, when all the Jews and most of the Arabs were dead, the German officials announced a press conference to be held at 3 o'clock in the morning. The press had to wait through a 45-minute speech before someone asked in desperation whether the hostages were alive or dead. The Executive Board of the IOC made this announcement later that day: 'The Olympic Games are proceeding for the sake of sport and sport only. All official receptions are cancelled. All ceremonies will be kept as simple as possible'. As if that was the only recognition of the disaster that was needed.

Yet this act took place within a sporting framework that had encompassed the participation of and also ignored the historic contribution made by, a Jewish team competing at one of the earliest Olympic Games, some 2,000 years before (albeit a team without women members).

The historical perspective

The majority of Jews at that time were becoming increasingly suspicious of the Hellenization of Israel, particularly as delegates to the Olympics were expected to take with them gifts for Hercules! There was a protest made at the 152nd Games, which were held simultaneously in Greece and at Tyre, when the Jewish contingent sent by Herod refused to donate to paganism.

Anyway, the end result was the uprising of the Jews against the armies of Alexander The Great, which is chronicled as the Maccabean War. The ensuing centuries of Jewish dispersion into other countries put the final block on any sporting aspirations as a race.

The concept of sport and recreation for pleasure rather than physical exercise taken to prevent ill health, or as preparation for self-defence, remained in the Jewish collective consciousness as alien as the Hellenic culture from which it had sprung. However, the Jews found themselves viewed with more than equal suspicion by their new hosts. With their movement restricted and forced to live within prescribed boundaries and not allowed to own land, ghetto living robbed the Jews of any chance of taking part in sport.

With a new enlightened age dawning towards the end of the nineteenth century, Jews were able to consider some sports as an option, particularly in the West. However, many sports clubs, particularly the more recreational and social golf and tennis clubs, barred Jews from membership. Jews began forming their own sports clubs. Within these organizations, women were at last able to take part. Although not many made it into the mainstream world of sport, those who did certainly made up for the rest.

In America, Elaine V. Rosenthal came second in the National Golf Championships in 1914, and Charlotte Epstein established swimming as a sport for all women, founding the American Women's Swimming Association in 1917. She was responsible for the inclusion of women's swimming events in the 1920 Olympics and was the US Olympic Team Manager in 1920, 1924 and 1932.

In Canada, Fanny (Bobbie) Rosenfeld played a great game of ice hockey, basketball and softball, and also tied for the women's world record 100-yard dash in 1925. After the 1928 Olympics, she was hailed by the Canadian press as the country's outstanding female athlete of the half century. Lily Kronenberger was the world's figure skating champion from 1908 to1911. And in 1935, a leading member of the USA Women's ski team was Alice Damrosch Wolf Kizer, who became the manager of the Olympic team in 1936.

The 1936 Summer Games were boycotted by the Palestine Olympic Committee as they were taking place in Nazi Germany.

Even though many tennis clubs in Britain refused membership to Jews, Angela Buxton still managed to be part of the winning doubles combination at Wimbledon in 1956. Prue Hyman captained the Women's Cricket Team at Oxford University and went on to become an England international.

Angela Buxton applied for membership of the All England Lawn Tennis Croquet Club immediately after the championships. In 1986, thirty years on, she wrote again asking them whether they had now considered her application. She received this reply: 'be patient'. . .

Even now, with the twentieth century drawing to its close, Jewish sports activity only seems to take place within the ethnic group.

Sporting associations

The Association of Jewish Youth in Great Britain, which is organized around ethnic youth club membership, puts on a full programme of events for girls and women. The directorate provides five-aside football tournaments and netball competitions, although they are not aware of any individual women having played outside of their league. Neither do they know whether any female track or field athletes have taken their talents into the mainstream of British sport.

In line with 'progressive' initiatives being taken by the colleges of physical education, state schools and local authority providers of sport and recreation, AJY are introducing mixed events. Male and female, not Jew and Gentile! Also taken on board are the moves towards emphasizing the principle of recreational participation rather than promoting competitive elitism!

In the Jewish historical context, this would seem a rather superfluous innovation. Unaware of the comic irony contained within his conversation with me, Julian Cohen, Sports Director of the British AJY said, 'Sport is now being projected as a vehicle for improving communicative qualities and for social interaction.' Within the confines of the Jewish community that apparently hoped for state of affairs is a *fait accomplis*. . .

Nevertheless, it should be mentioned that there are 150 clubs with a huge membership, and we must hope that these will produce some mainstream sportswomen in the future.

There is another sporting movement in modern Jewish culture, called Maccabi. This again is primarily a youth club organization, but of a more orthodox and religious kind. It used to be called the Federation of Jewish Societies, *Die Judische Turnerschaft*, until 1921. When you consider that the far more liberal AJY don't organize any games on the Sabbath, it's remarkable that Maccabi exists at all.

Maccabi hold an international Games called the Maccabiah in Israel every four years. Some call it the Jewish Olympics, and have done so since its inception in 1932.

In 1970 there were 40,000 athletes affiliated to sports organizations in Israel. However, of this number, 15,000 were in school sport, 13,000 registered with the football association (we can assume these are all male) 9,000 in basketball (some women do play) and the rest are to be found in tennis, judo and some other minority sports.

Israel itself has endeavoured to integrate itself into Asian sport which I don't see as a very positive step. The Asian people as a group, particularly those of the Moslem tradition, tend to keep themselves within their own shtetls*, and they are extremely unsporting in their attitudes towards women.

Physical restraints

How can we expect any religious dogma, designed by men for the benefit of men, to yield sufficient space to the concept of women taking delight in the physical nature of their own bodies?

Orthodox Judaism still requires women to shave their heads after marriage, substitute unattractive, usually mid-brown, wigs and to cover themselves up generally — what price swimming or running? In much the same way, and largely for the same reason, Moslem beliefs decree that the women in their group should wear body-hiding garments (chadors) bearing a striking resemblance to those of catholicism's nuns. Hardly attire conducive to participation in a game of hockey — and netball could get interesting too . . .

When the Indian women's cricket team toured here they wore trousers, not just because they were the more sensible clothes for their sport, but because they are not allowed to show their legs in public.

One could perhaps be forgiven for missing the point of the development in densely Asian — populated areas — of women-only sports activities such as swimming. One 'women-only' session was provided by local authority at the request of a few slightly liberated Sikh women. The feminist women's liberation advocates are often the instigators of women-only sport and recreation sessions. They know that many women in our western culture, who are new to the idea that women may enjoy physical leisure-time pursuits, might be reluctant to parade ineptitude before well-

*Jewish villages — ghettos.

practised, and therefore more skilful, male onlookers. At least in each others' company, most healthy-minded western females don't object to wearing appropriate sportswear, unlike the women restricted and constrained by male rules of propriety who attend the sports centre pool, the majority of whom remained fully clothed in the water until the instructor repeatedly remonstrated with them. Because there are no such restrictions in the wider community, other women can attend the swimming pool at anytime they choose, whether its for half an hour after school with their children or a weekend evening with their friends.

Those of us involved in women's sport find ourselves on the horns of a dilemma. We have to weigh up respect for cultures that are different from our own against the urgent need to free all women from male domination — the best way, of course, being through sport.

Into Africa

The so-called Third World also discriminates against itself. Although Africa, once called the Dark Continent, has only been open to scrutiny for just over 100 years or so, it is still woefully behind the times. With clitoridectomy in full swing, I doubt those mutilated women have much instinct for the hunt left in them.

The only women likely to participate in sport or represent their respective countries are those of the town-dwelling middle classes or are women who are numbered among the thousands of expatriate Africans including the 40,000 living in the United States, those holding British passports and the 11,000 studying in the USSR.

One must consider the outstanding achievement of Narwal El Moutawakil from Morocco, who wiped the floor with all her competitors in the 400 metres hurdles in the 1984 Olympics in 54.61 seconds, while she attended the Iowa State University.

There has as we know been a tremendous influence emanating throughout the 51 countries south of the Sahara from the Arabic regions of the North.

These countries are all demagogic male-chauvinist states. In what would be perceived as ordinary, civilized circumstances, physical recreational activity for women is made somewhat more difficult through the onset of pregnancy and child rearing. In Africa generally these factors are multiplied by the drastic social and economic situation facing most women, with birth control denounced by some heads of state as moral decadence. And this by leaders who see no moral decadence in waging endless tribal war, or allowing innocent millions to be sentenced to death from malnutrition and related causes before they are five years old, a direct result of their inept governmental economic lack of strategy and organization.

These leaders govern people whose natural life expectancy in most areas is no more than thirty-five years, with 50 per cent of the entire African population aged under fifteen!

When Masai women in Kenya feel that they must give birth to fifteen or sixteen children in the hope that some of them may live to adulthood, and that all the premature deaths from diarrhoea, caused by having no clean water and an inadequate diet are either pronounced to be 'God's will' or 'Evil Spirits', depending on which religious doctrines they adhere to, it may seem that female excellence or even participation in fun, physical activities called sport, are a little too remote from a literally blinding reality. Trachoma is a common virus infection of the eye which is treatable at most stages with drugs but which, left alone, will cause permanent blindness. What chance of treatment when there is only one doctor serving over 25,600 people and only one psychiatrist for every two million?

However, there are some Kenyan women who are able to make the most of any opportunity offered and have actually represented their country in sport abroad. Women like Ruth Waithera, who took part in the Olympic 400 metres in Los Angeles after winning the 100-, 200- and 400-metre races in the National Championships. The other ten Kenyan women who also became national champions in that Olympic year should be regarded as real heroines and have their names inscribed on the women's world sports roll of honour. In case you don't know their names, here they are.

In the 800m Justina Chepchirchir; 1,500m Mary Chepkemboi; 3,000m Helen Kimaiyo; 100m hurdles Frida Kiptala; 400m hurdles, Rose Tata; high jump, R. Chepkoech; long jump, Pemina Akama; shot putt, Herina Malit; discus, Phillis Macharia; and javelin, Milka Johnson.

Most sports-minded people remember Kip Keno for his long-distance performances, but what of Esther Kiplagat, the 10,000-metre runner, or Alice Okello, 10,000-metre race walker and Mercy Nyambura, noted for the 10-kilometre road walk?

Two African countries that were never colonialized by Europeans or 'whites' are Liberia and Ethiopia.

Even though Liberia had the kind of environment that could seem amenable to women's sports, no women seem to represent Liberia in international competition and therefore Liberian women's sports activities are not chronicled here. This is a country on the West coast that was settled by returning freed American slaves in the mid nineteenth century. Universal suffrage was included in their constitution. A few years ago, the civilized façade, waving precariously like their flags of convenience, was torn down. The then President Tolbert was savagely murdered while he lay in his bed, and thereafter his body became the butt of a catcalling mob. Universal suffering, more like.

Ethiopia's sporting claim to fame is by virtue of its male long-distance runners, and it maintains a strong presence in African sport generally.

Not long ago, a large group of Jews of the tribe called Falashas (or 'strangers') by the Ethiopians, and persecuted as such, were airlifted through the Sudan to Israel. I would expect that, tradition permitting and modern times and society enlightening, some of the women or at least their children will take part in sport both in Israel and elsewhere.

Liberia's neighbour, the Ivory Coast, is a relatively wealthy country by African standards. It even has the only ice rink outside of South Africa — at least that is a start. And, although they do not have any skating champions yet, in July 1984 at the African championships in Morocco, Ms Tenin Camara won the javelin event with a throw of 45.48m.

In 1975, the year that gave us sex equality in Britain, by way of parliamentary legislation in Somalia, the President also decreed that men and women were equal. While I enjoyed my new-found legal equality by racing against a male Olympic skater, Paul French, on a sheet of frozen water called Baston Fen, ten Moslem scholars disagreed with the Somalian President and said that the Koran categorically states that women are inferior. In the interests of equality, President Barre had them executed. Official equality for Somalian woman, however theoretical, remained. In country areas — which of course are most areas — the only sport on offer to many Somali women is that of spending eight hours a day flapping their arms in the middle of a field to keep the birds off the crops. Medals could perhaps be struck in commemoration of a new sports discipline!

There is no point in ever more elaboration on the social, economic and political factors that manifest themselves in Africa today to show how the majority of women are deprived by them of any existence much higher than that of a cow. But neither can we ignore them, or South Africa.

The politics of sport

If the history of the demise of colonial rule points a finger to the future and if the Afrikaaner tribal rulers and despots disappear from the scene there, we may assume that the new black tribal authorities will, as they did in Uganda, kick out or oppress the merchant, professional and clerical classes (who are mainly Asians or 'coloured') and South Africa will quickly become another Ghana, Guinea or Tanzania. I would hold out not much greater hope for the future comfort of the 120,000 Jews now in residence. Unless, perhaps, the more moderate voice of the 40 per cent English-speaking whites of British origin is heard.

Meanwhile, although South Africa appears to have the only real opportunity for the development and pursuit of women's sports — black *or* white — in the whole of the huge African continent, this is not taking place. The reason is, of course, the political dogma which states that people of different races, that is colours, may not legally associate with each other socially, and so sport is yet another Afrikaans area with 'separate development' built in.

Until 1948, and the election of a Nationalist Afrikaan government, racial discrimination was a social practice only. It latterly became entrenched with successive acts of parliament.

Those of us living in countries which have inalienable rights to equal citizenship, may well refuse to accept that sport can possibly be an instrument of political manoeuvre.

One only has to consider something as obvious as the chagrin of Hitler, that advocate of Aryan supremacy, when the black American Jesse Owens beat the Nazi contingent at the Munich bierfest/Olympics in 1936. Sport in itself is not political and yet if finds itself used by the unscrupulous to emphasize political points of view. How many times do we hear advocates of male supremacy quote slower times, less height, less length in sports events to buoy up spurious argument, ignoring the fact that in the lower and middle ranges of ability the differences are minimal. And what of the myth of black athleticism, a leftover vestige of the slave trade perhaps, when Africans were measured by their strength — note, in this case, there are no divisions made between male and female! If any contest is not open to all human beings that wish to take part, my judgement as a referee would be to declare a 'no contest'.

There has been an increasingly common tendency by both right-wing and left-wing politicians to make sport a political issue. A group of British Tory politicians provoked an outcry with a pamphlet stating that, if Labour council candidates were elected they would prohibit young boys from playing football in school and they would have to play netball instead. It was even deemed worthy of comment by the Chairman of the Sports Council at an event held to present the Sports Journalist of the Year award. What had been politically left out was the rest of the L.E.A. directive — and it was a suggestion only — that football *and* netball should be available as sporting options for both boys *and* girls.

Sport has always been seen as an ambassador for its country, and national teams are assumed to be representative of any country's population. The representation of South Africa would, by their own definition if it contained people of different colours, be described as 'multi-national'. So, therefore, there is no national representation without apartheid. At least in Britain a team comprising Welsh, Scottish, Irish and English would be called the Great British National Team. This would encompass all skin complexions and all religious creeds.

The situation for women in South Africa is much the same as in any Western industrialized and automated society except that, unless there is special dispensation, black women and white women are segregated. If you looked at a pile of cast off, sweaty sports kit I doubt whether you would be able to tell what colour the previous wearers were. But, in taking a stand on apartheid, other nations risk penalizing the 'innocent' with the guilty. Of about 12,000 registered black women netball players in South Africa and 40,000 whites, none were able to play in the netball world games held in Glasgow 1987.

Divide and rule?

In general, any practice which seeks to divide human beings into manageable or governable chunks, should be viewed with some suspicion, but benign global government recedes even further into the realms of science fiction when those in authority, whether they be democratically elected or self-elected, divide people into ever smaller groups.

The campaign which seeks to bring about the destruction of apartheid by means of economic sanctions or penalities imposed upon those who will dally with it, including bans in the field of sport, is now challenged from within black South Africa itself.

An alternative solution to the problem of abolition of racial discrimination is gaining ground. This is a Zulu-led campaign for multi-racial power-sharing in South Africa which will hold more charm than the ANC for those who believe that apartheid can be destroyed by non-violent means.

This new organization, which seeks to merge the white-ruled province of Natal with the Bantustan or black homeland of Kwa Zulu, is asking liberal support for diplomatic pressure to be brought to bear for the release of Mandela and the scrapping of the Group Areas Act which separates the people's domiciles according to racial origin. This organization might well offer a more pleasant and seemingly more civilized way of contributing to a more guilt-free international conscience with its eschewal of all sanctions, including sport.

A balance of power, an equality between black and white, man and woman, must come about. However, there is no other way, except than by a military-style coup, that the black majority in South Africa will ever by allowed to govern the land that, to a large extent, belongs to the only white African tribe, the Afrikaaner. They have nowhere else to go, they have lived in Africa for more than 300 years and they are going to have to accommodate other tribal influences in their parliament or face destruction. Equality is the only viable solution, in politics as in sport.

The movement of women or the women's movement

One of the biggest drawbacks to women's development and subsequent liberation whether in South Africa or elsewhere, is the problem of migration.

Although, traditionally, African women are expected to work the land, while the men do the 'hunting', prevailing economic and social factors dictate both in South Africa and in other African countries that the women are largely left behind in the poor country areas, while men go and hunt for money in the towns, large farms or plantations.

For instance: just above Zambia and Mozambique on the east coast is Tanzania, where a ready source of money is liquor-making, particularly at harvest time. There is a beer called Komoni, made from fermented maize flour which is produced by village women. Because of the relatively large amounts of money to be earned by turning crops into alcohol rather than using them as food, particularly in view of constant food shortages, the men put pressure on the women to produce drink, and thereafter line their own pockets with the ill-gotten gains. Most of any family's food supply depends on what the women can produce from the land on which they are expected to stay. It is interesting to note that, should a woman complain that the volume of work is too great, a man will take another wife! Not much room for tender loving care between heterosexuals there. It is reported that there are some women's group meetings being organized around these common problems in Tanzanian villages, but no decisions can actually be implemented without the sanction of the men — so progress is going to be very slow, unless central government takes issue with the ignorant and greedy exploiters of a monetary system that depends on women's subservience.

The men in these cases are voluntarily mobile, taking their own or at least their women's money with them into the more prosperous and modern environments of nearby towns.

Migration forced upon them by poor living conditions has its own human emotional problem. When, as need dictates, men leave women and children to the mammoth task of keeping themselves alive on pieces of barren ground, they often take a second woman, and consequently children, in the environs of the work they have found elsewhere.

In highly industrialized and technologically advanced societies there is still an acceptance of women working on a static and home-rooted basis while men 'migrate' daily, weekly or even monthly to their areas of work. One of the factors, often the greatest outside of social stricture, that works against women's participation in sport is poverty, which is *always* accompanied by physical and mental debility.

Not having the power within their own countries to institute agricultural and technological advance, which might make those countries self-sufficient and able to support an increasing population, the women of the Caribbean chose to migrate themselves.

It is not surprising that many of these Caribbean migrant women in the USA, Canada and Britain are in the vanguard of women's liberation. Neither is it surprising that these women and their descendants are among the best, or at least most active, in women's sport.

The women's national sport in the West Indies is netball and there is great rivalry between the islands. Although Jamaica and Trinidad have the largest memberships to their respective national organizations, it does not prevent small islands such as St Vincent from enjoying competition to the full. As my adopted sister Juliette remembers from her schooldays spent there: 'The Jamaican girls used to come over and squash us! For years I imagined all Jamaican women were giants because of the size of the girls that used to play in their international teams.' However, its that other ex-British colony that heads the world's women's netball tables — Australia. Following them are New Zealand, Trinidad & Tobago, then England and Jamaica.

In passing, Australia and its booming economy, would seem to be the demonstrable truth that emancipation and prosperity does the most to promote women's sport, and also shows the discrepancies that occur in female representation where there are disadvantaged groups. There are few women of Aborigine origin at international level. International contests are the ultimate aim in competitive sports, therefore, as it is a process of selection from lowest level through to the highest, with National Body selection boards as the last hurdle to be leapt, it would seem the fairest indication of policy.

To return to the Caribbean: at the 41st Annual Conference of the Federation of Women's Institutes, the Prime Minister of Trinidad & Tobago, Mr ANR Robinson, stated publicly that his government places great emphasis on the special role and responsibilities of women who have, he said, traditionally carried more than their fair share of the burden in both Trinidad and Tobago and in Caribbean society as a whole. He reiterated that women must participate fully in the political process, while pointing out that many people still feel that politics is not for women. He said that he did not share that view.

Trinidad and Tobago have a woman minister for sport, youth, culture and creative arts, Ms Jennifer Johnson.

I quote here from a manifesto which is the basis of the present government. . .

'They [women] form a significant economic source which has

remained dormant over the years. The dynamism and creative energies that abound in our population of women must be given all the avenues, outlets and opportunities to improve their social conditions and to carry our nation forward.'

Available land space not precluding, if you feel like rushing out to take advantage of the pleasant climate both politically, socially and geographically, you could do worse than jump on a plane to Trinidad, or even Barbados where netball is the number one sport for women, with clubs thriving at all levels, and many playing to a high national standard.

Encouragement for so-called minority or oppressed groups of women to take up their options for sport and recreation exists within the framework of the women's sports initiatives taken by women themselves outside of, but sometimes resourced by, government both local and federal. In Britain, Canada, the USA, Australia, and even Japan (not noted for it's female emancipation in its tea-house-littered, geisha girl past) there are local and national, voluntary, self-promoting and self-supporting women's sports associations, foundations and federations.

These are the organizations which will bring all women who love sport together, and will do more for minority participation than any other. Our strength is in our differences. What is needed is plenty of endurance and stomach for hard work, and we all know from our own experience that women have plenty of that!

CHAPTER EIGHT
The Food Factor

A little knowledge is a dangerous thing — but not for some producers of food supplements. Break someone's diet down to its constituent chemical parts, tell her that, due to pressurized living, she's missing something or other and then sell her a packet of that something or other at a good price and, hey presto — you're rich. They'll ask 'why bother to boil spinach any more when you can take a tablet?' — although I wouldn't use a Popeye cartoon as an incentive to spinach-eating, since Olive Oyl never gets so much as half a leaf. Perhaps we should create a female cartoon character who performs great feats after cooking and eating a nutritionally balanced meal!

There is no substitute for a properly balanced diet and no way that women can perform well, either at recreational exercise level or top-level competition, unless they are properly nourished.

For example, consider the reasons for the low level of single-parent participation in many of the new, often women-only initiatives taken by forward-looking and caring local authorities. Chief amongst them is the low level of nourishment, giving rise to the tiredness and depression that many of these women suffer from, because they are living on miserably low allowances paid them by the State for bringing up the next generation of work-force and voters.

There are many long screeds devoted to telling women what they ought to eat and what constitutes a balanced diet, but what is needed is a simple explanatory sheet on how they can make the best use of the food they buy and consume, written in plain language distributed in mother and baby clinics, doctors', waiting rooms and all the other places where the attendance of women is high.

A healthy diet plan

The Americans, as usual, have come up with a good plan. As early as 1956, their Department of agriculture developed a 'Four Food Group Plan' for adequate nutrition. They grouped foods according to their predominant nutritional value rather than the more obscure scientific systems.

These groups are made up thus:

1. fruit and vegetables
2. cereal and grains
3. high protein (fish, poultry, beans, eggs)
4. milk and dairy products.

It was suggested that active women need *at least* four servings from each of these groups, and that 'sedentary' women only need two servings from group 2 and 3 — the most expensive — and four from groups 1 and 2 — the cheapest. How does that work out in the course of a real day?

A serving in this instance means half a cup of fruit or vegetables, one slice of bread or half a cup of cooked cereal or one cup of dry ready-to-eat cereal; 2-3 ounces, cooked weight, from the protein group (eg one cupful of cooked beans); and one cup of milk and 1-2 ounces of cheese or butter from the last group.

Using the plan as a guide, breakfast would be one bowl of cereal with half a cup of milk on it, accompanied by one slice of buttered bread and one cup of tea or coffee made with water and milk.

Lunch could be one cup of cooked beans on one slice of buttered toast with two pieces of fruit and a glass of milk.

For dinner you could then eat 6 ounces of fish, poultry or meat or another cupful of baked beans plus two 4-ounce portions of vegetables topped with a knob of butter and cheese. Pudding would then be a piece of fruit. One assumes a little raw cane sugar would be acceptable.

The only extra mineral requirement is iron and calcium, particularly if you don't eat fish, meat or poultry. The iron from these is absorbed far more readily than from vegetable sources. Women need 18 mg of iron a day during menstration and 12mg at other times in the month. You needn't show up as anaemic to need iron. Iron is stored in your bone marrow, liver and other tissues and this reserve is used up before the other 50 per cent of the iron in your blood cells drops noticeably.

Iron deficiency can make you tired more easily during any exertion because iron delays the removal of lactic acid from your muscles.

Lack of calcium is another culprit — if you drink 1 pint of milk, eat a carton of yoghurt, 1 ounce of cheddar and an ice-cream every day, you will be getting your 1,000mg requirement. If you are not, you should consider changing your diet, or take a calcium supplement but only enough to bring you to that ordinary level of consumption.

If you do not menstruate, you should look for more calcium in your diet (about 500mg more) as the lack of the hormone oestrogen causes calcium loss from bone. Two glasses of milk contain 500mg.

Supplements for sportswomen?

As for all these high-protein supplements, they are not going to increase your muscle size by magic, and if you overdose on protein, your liver will break it down as best it can because your body has no capacity to store extra protein and will excrete it as organic acid and ammonia in your urine. This condition will make you pass water more frequently and will dehydrate you during your exercise.

If you are actually in hard training, one cup of cooked beans a day will add as much protein to your diet as you need. Even in a super strength-building weight-training programme, you do not need that much extra protein to build muscles. If you are putting on 8 ounces of muscle every week, you are only adding 2 ounces of protein to your body mass or just over ¼ ounce a day!

You can enlarge and strengthen your muscles just by exercising them against resistance. You don't even need to eat to do this, although fasting is a dangerous way to prove any theory.

And what about salt! Many women now avoid it like the plague as it's known that too much salt in the bloodstream can cause clotting which in turn can lead to kidney failure, a stroke or a heart attack. However, as long as you are eating a reasonable diet, you won't need to worry about salt replacement, even if you perspire freely and heavily during exercise. Some women take salt tablets before strenuous activity because they think it will prevent cramp. All that they are likely to do is cause nausea! People generally absorb far too much salt in their diet anyway, as most processed food manufacturers use it both in the flavouring and in the preserving process. A tin of peas, for example, would supply just the same amount of salt and nausea as a tablet before any competition.

Cramp during exercise or towards the end of it is usually due to insufficient oxygen from your blood supply. Although cramp in early exercise may be due to a mineral imbalance such as calcium, sodium or potassium deficiency, excess salt (sodium) levels are a very rare cause, although calcium abnormality can be caused by overdosing on vitamin D.

Cramp is far more likely to respond to increased fluid consumption than to anything else, so if you drink a small glass of water before you start any physical effort and at twenty-minute intervals during it, you should escape cramp from muscular oxygen starvation.

'Sports'-type drinks often contain sugar, but as sugar delays absorption of the drink into your bloodstream, your stomach will stay full longer.

Some years ago, one of my club mates arrived at a training session with a crate of highly concentrated glucose drinks and told us all that he'd found a secret success formula. All we had to do was drink a bottle each and we would notice the difference by the end of that session. We all glugged as much of it down as we could, although it was rather filling, and got on the ice for a warm-up line out — this is where a group of speed skaters sit in behind one another and rhythmically skate round the middle of the 111.12m track for 2-3,000 metres.

As we didn't eat for the prescribed two or three hours before training, our tummies were pretty empty and, as I went round the top corner for the second time, I seemed to feel the bottleful of syrupy liquid I'd drunk slop ominously against my ribs. As I got down to the next corner, I hopped off to the loo, where I stayed for about five minutes.

Coming back out to the ice pad, I was amazed to see that it was virtually empty of speed skaters. They gradually came tottering out of the gents' toilet with surprised expressions on their faces. Afterwards, we found out that this was a high-density drink meant to be sipped from time to time to replenish blood sugar levels in our muscles. None of us ever bothered with dietary supplements after that. They do more harm than good if you are careless about the doses.

Lots of women take vitamin pills on board, but vitamins are absorbed naturally while eating a good diet of the kind that I have described, and you don't really need extra to help you exercise and take part in sport and recreational activity generally.

Four vitamins are used in the breakdown of carbohydrates and protein thiamin (B_1), niacin, riboflavin (B_2) and pantothenic acid, and these are all present in your breakfast cereal bowl.

Even extra vitamin C doesn't stay in your body very long — 80 per cent of a 1g dose passes out in your water shortly after you have swallowed it.

If you are looking to store some extra glycogen in your muscles — commonly called carbohydrate loading — just some extra pasta, bread or cake will do.

The very best way to increase your endurance is by depleting your stores of blood sugar by training so hard that you hit the wall of fatigue once a week during training, then doing it three days before competition and couple this with a reduced training programme for that three days prior to the event. If you eat your usual diet but include some extra carbohydrate content, this should give you the boost that you want in the most natural way.

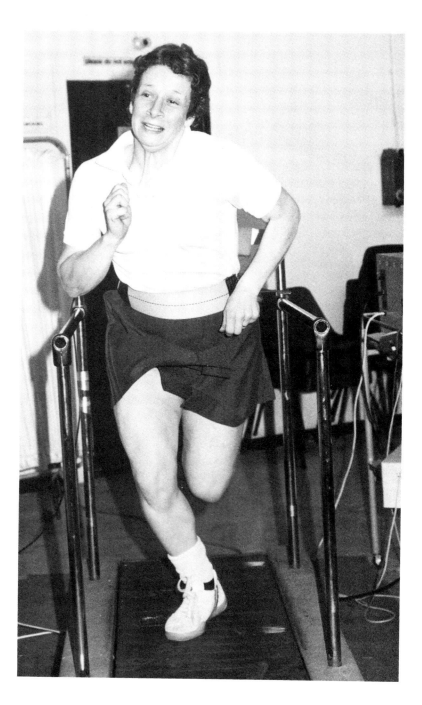

CHAPTER NINE

Training — an end in itself?

'It will be all right on the night' is an optimism that applies as much to sporting events as it does to the theatre rehearsals that spawned it. Training can be as exhilarating and pleasurable as any one single event or competition. It can be even more so for those of us who prefer to travel hopefully, rather than face what might well seem to some to be a disappointing arrival. After all, only one side or one person can win and that leaves an awful lot of runners-up.

Training can prepare us for all the other eventualities in life, as well as its more obvious application to sports activities.

The weaker sex?

Women have always suffered from the implication that we are the weaker sex — even though, at the present time, 90 per cent of the wealth produced by the under-developed countries, termed the 'Third World' by sociologists and those who don't live in it, is from the sweated labour of women and girls.

There has always been at least a double standard for us, which is defined by class. The picture of an oft idealized Victorian-type middle- or upper-class woman dabbing her forehead with cologne after a little exertion, contrasts sharply with that of women heaving coal carts around down the mines.

Those detractors of female strength who quote our physiological and biological differences in support of their theories, would do well to mug up on relevant data for female endurance levels. These are in reality linked in to our female body systems.

Because of the feminizing hormone oestrogen we lay down more fat than men and therefore it takes us longer to deplete our stores of energy. Most women can be good at sport and recreational activity with a minimum of extra training, particularly where their energy output is to be of a sustained and regular nature, with occasional spurts required here and there. They have to train that much harder for the short sharp bursts such as the 500-metre ice speed skating race; although, if this is introduced as an interval in a training programme so that it becomes a repetitive effort, a woman is more likely to sustain that effort than a male co-trainee. (This is a real beast of an example as a 500-metre short track race at maximum energy output can take as little as fifty seconds for a top female and forty-six for a top male. Imagine having to do that four times in quick succession, even with sixty-second rests!)

How much to train?

If you are looking for an average exercise programme that will do you the most good, you should train for about twenty-five minutes, three times a week. If you want to take a somewhat more serious approach to your level of physical fitness you should increase your exercise to a nearly daily routine.

The art of training for any sport is to acquire strength of mind and body integrated with the skill and technique needed for your sports event.

The bottom line for an improvement in your general health and feelings of well-being would be to train for around twenty-five minutes, three times a week. After thirty minutes working out there is a slower rate of improvement and, equally, the increase in performance level slows down after three such sessions in any seven-day period. You can safely assume that any regular exercise will improve your muscular endurance and give you a stronger heart.

I have included at the end of this chapter my patent twenty-eight day training cycle, based on the studies on menstruation in athletes and sportswomen by Dr Katherina Dalton. What I *haven't* included in that is the new-fangled scientific way for finding out if you're out of breath, very out of breath, or dying! This is called aerobic monitoring and here follows how it's done.

You are fit when, after a five-minute training session which has taken you to your 'target heart rate', your pulse drops by thirty beats a minute after the first minute of rest. If, like me, you are no good at maths, especially when sweat is dribbling into your eyes and your nose is running, the next bit could put you off training and physical activity and effort for life.

It's no good taking your pulse for the whole of that second minute because your pulse will slow down far more at the end of it than at the start. So you multiply your heart rate by twelve in the first five seconds of rest during that first minute immediately after you cease the exercise. Again multiply by twelve for the last five seconds of the second minute's pulse count — got that? Good! *Then* you subtract the second number from the first and this gives you your recovery pulse rate.

The fitter you get, the nearer to the magic thirty beat drop you'll get. (A fit heart rate is approximately 120 beats a minute during exercise.)

To note the strengthening of your heart, you can calculate a rate called the heart rate reserve. This is done by taking the figure 220 and subtracting your age. This gives you your maximum heart rate. Mine should be 174. You then subtract the resting heart rate. The resting heart rate is your pulse rate when you wake up in the morning before you get out of bed — call that 70. This makes my heart rate reserve 105. You then divide that heart rate reserve figure by two and then add on your resting heart rate, to give you your target heart rate. This comes to 127.5 for me and that's my problem!

The actual aim is to achieve a target heart rate, which is usually about 120 anyway for all adults, male or female, for a period of ten minutes within any training session, and this will strengthen your heart.

The true meaning of aerobic exercise is any physical sustained effort that delivers an adequate or near-adequate supply of oxygen to your body.

Anaerobic exercise is not a rival commercial cult set up to combat aerobic dance classes, but is that level of effort that leads to the accumulation of lactic acid in the bloodstream because of lack of oxygen. The point of endurance training is that the more you train, the greater the effort that you will be able to make before incurring the pain and discomfort of oxygen debt. Fortunately, this condition does not need the use of sums to evaluate it.

You can train your body to tolerate some of the discomfort and raise its anaerobic threshold by hard interval training. The snag is that the high levels of lactic acid will make you tire more easily, so it's best not to overdo this kind of work in an average training session. There's no real point in going over this threshold more than two or three times a week.

You can plan interval training even during a jog around city streets — between lamp posts, for instance. You jog from the first one to the second, run from the second to the third and walk from the third to fourth and repeat. You'll soon find out where the halfway mark is; if you go beyond what I call the point of no return, you'll have to get a bus back or phone someone for a lift.

The trainer

What about that solitary and much abused figure in the background — the coach? This is the one who volunteered for that vast army of unpaid instructors and the best of these have come through their own sport. Loaded with the knowledge of how it's done, they have set about passing on their expertise instead of leaving the sport when they are no longer able or wish to compete. In this way also, the coach will continue in an established social network that will have been built up over many years and will also maintain a reasonable level of self-fitness into old age as well.

Coaches need not have been top-flight competitors. They are very often participants of average ability, with a good grasp of problem areas, which they have often already worked out good ways of overcoming.

They do need to have a compassionate personality so that they can bring understanding with them to an activity that will hold disappointments and frustrations as well as joy for the participant. The ability to motivate perseverance is an essential prerequisite in any activity that demands high levels of skill, agility and technique. This does not mean that a drill sergeant mentality should be tolerated, however.

The coach should also have the ability to spot and encourage specially talented participants and have the selfless initiative to pass these people on to more highly able coaches if and when it becomes necessary.

If all these inherent and acquired qualities and skills sound familiar to you, it may be that you are recognizing female/feminine traits.

Every amateur and professional sport has its own governing body and any coach has to start from the basis of knowing the rules and regulations. These often incorporate the safety factors which are so important, as well as ensuring that participants or competitors don't get themselves disqualified or hurt out of ignorance. Whether it's an offside rule which results in the other side gaining an advantage, a dangerous tackle in a penalty area which could allow the other team to score more easily, or impeding another athlete on a track which could ultimately lose them the race, it's the coach's responsibility.

The funniest incident I can recall on the international ice speed circuit was when I disqualified a young woman who I clearly saw punch the girl next to her on the track as they came belting down the last but one straight. I was confronted by this skater and her parents immediately after the decision was announced and I was amazed to hear her insist in very good English that it had been 'self defence'. Her coach had obviously been teaching her from a different rule book.

Of course, the traditional single-sex sports like lacrosse, hockey and netball have plenty of women coaches, but once you enter the twilight zone inhabited by the old male-orientated sports, such as football and ice hockey, you have a sudden dearth of female coaches. This is not because the women don't have the talent, but women coached by men seem to fall foul of the still unfortunately prevalent social mores of male authoritarianism. Even when they become proficient, they still lack the self-confidence to take the proverbial bull by the horns and take control of their own competence, which is often considerable.

If it is accepted that unless you have taken part in a sport or recreational activity you cannot coach it, then surely by the same token unless you are a woman you cannot train women.

Training and pregnancy

One of the most obvious areas of concern for women between the years of puberty and the menopause is menstruation and pregnancy and how this affects our ability to take part in sport and recreational activities at all levels and of all kinds.

These are very important shared areas of concern for all sportswomen, whether as participant, coach, instructor, teacher or organizer.

I remember when I was in training and still racing, a doctor asked me why I wouldn't take the contraceptive Pill. When I gave her my reasons (in those days the Pill had a high oestrogen content) and added that I felt that taking the Pill would slow me down, she said, 'Not as much as being pregnant'. I told her then that my gut reaction was to say that her opinion was rubbish. There is now an increasing trend, medically substantiated, towards viewing pregnancy and subsequent delivery as the ultimate aerobic resistance training, with mothers such as marathon runner Ingrid Kristiansen and Mary Decker Slaney, the world mile record holder, being cited as examples.

If you agree that having a baby satisfies the criteria for endurance training and that it thereafter increases your strength and fitness levels, there is no point in worrying unduly about training going to waste while you are pregnant.

In any case, you should do nothing that incurs an oxygen debt or that diverts blood to your skin and muscle, away from other organs such as your liver, kidney and uterus. Even though the baby has a separate blood supply, it is dependent on yours for filtering the nutrients it needs, a process which takes place in the uterus. There are no definite results as yet for determining how little oxygen a developing foetus can stand without risk.

I used to skate as usual for the first few weeks of pregnancy, but after about eight weeks I'd slow down and start to cut down on the number of laps. At around twelve weeks, I would begin to take it very easy indeed in training terms. I decided that for me, the time to stop was when I felt that I would get out of breath if I continued and if I wanted to sit down after a couple of laps at a medium pace. Thereafter, I would only skate in a totally recreational manner. Mind you, I think that all this wisdom came with age, as when I was seventeen and seven months pregnant, I remember the ice rink manager clearing the ice for me so that I could do a couple of fast laps in my smock — I hasten to add that this was a one-off occasion!

With my other children, I gave up extra exercise when I was around sixteen weeks pregnant. You can still do all those nice little activities like relaxation exercises, you can use a hand grip and you can revolve your feet first in one direction and then in the other (all this while lying down — lovely!). Then you can pick up after your six-week postnatal check-up and get going again with renewed zest and vigour. Looking after small children is aerobic exercise bordering on the anaerobic.

Training and motherhood

If you want to continue your physical sports and recreational pursuits after you've had a child and you don't have a built-in baby sitter, there are quite a few options open to women. In Britain, many local authorities run sports sessions for women, most of them through the Action Sports Development programme, that provide crèche facilities, as do some right-minded sport and leisure centres. The leisure and recreation department of your local authority, usually located at the Town or City Hall, will have a list of such providers, and so should your local library.

The other alternative is to organize your own group through a mother and toddler's club, so that you can have a baby-sitting rota. A different mother could sit out each session. This gives a whole new meaning to the expression 'time out'!

Sports Council Regional Offices are listed on page 00 and their information offices will be able to put you in touch with the right organization. The Women's Sports Foundation contact numbers and addresses are also given on page 122.

Briefing

This training schedule is based on the natural twenty-eight-day cycle. It takes account of the variation in body weight and the sensations most of us experience during any one month. We can adapt it easily to our own specific needs, and benefit most, by starting on Mild Week One — Day 1 — four days before the next period is due. You could begin to peak around Medium Week Two — Day 4.

There might be a slight fall off in performance during Hard Week Three, after days 5 or 6, which, after the rest day, graduate into Medium Week Four, and eases into Mild Week One again.*

Do not forget to eat at the *end* of each set *not* before! Otherwise you will suffer from what I call the cereal or chewed chip in the throat syndrome. Another word of warning: if you have never previously used weights I suggest that you find a local sports facility with a multigym and proper supervision before you begin at home. If you cycle, either invest in cycling shorts, or sew window cleaning chamois leathers on the top inside legs and backside of ordinary track suit bottoms to prevent soreness.

WEEK		DAY 1 WARM UP	SOLID WORK	DAY 2 WARM UP	SOLID WORK	DAY 3 WARM UP	SOLID WORK	DAY 4 WARM UP	SOLID WORK	DAY 5 WARM UP	SOLID WORK	DAY 6 WARM UP	SOLID WORK	DAY 7
1	AM													REST
1	PM													
2	AM													REST
2	PM													
3	AM													REST
3	PM													
4	AM													REST
4	PM													

Mild week one

Mornings

1 Jog slowly on the spot, or around the room for 2 minutes.

2 Standing with feet apart, briskly bend your right knee, swinging your right arm backwards. Then, as you straighten your right leg, bend the knee of your left leg and straighten your right leg. Swinging your right arm across and your left arm behind you effectively shifting your body weight over the bent knee. Do this 10 times.

3 Lying flat with your back on the floor, pull your knees up to your chest, gently straighten them over your head to touch the floor behind it. Hold for 3-5 seconds, then bring your legs back slowly to the starting position flat on the floor. Repeat 5 times.

4 Squat in a crouched position on the floor, feet slightly apart with your left hand on your left foot, right hand on your right foot. Slowly rise, sliding your hands up your legs as you do so. Repeat 5 times.

5 Standing straight, stretch up your arms, then relax. Repeat 5 times.

Run for 5 minutes or cycle for 10 minutes or weight train for 10 minutes. Alternatively complete with 50 per cent of your normal schedule, where this would be more than the time given above.

Evenings

1 Jog for 2 minutes.

2 Standing straight, with feet apart, arms by your sides, gradually move your right hand down the side of your right leg as far past the knee as you can keeping your back straight. Straighten up and repeat with your left side. Repeat 10 times.

3 Sitting on the floor with feet apart, touch your left foot with your right hand, then sit up again. Now touch your right foot with your left hand and sit up. Repeat this 10 times.

4 Laying full length on the floor, flat on your back, arms by your sides, draw your knees slowly up to your chest, then return slowly, straightening your legs until you return to your original position. Repeat 10 times.

Skip for 5 minutes or 50 per cent of your usual time where this would be more.

Medium week two

Mornings

1 Jog gently on the spot or around the room for 3 minutes.

2 Standing with feet apart, briskly throw your arms out to the side at shoulder level. Bending your elbows, briskly bring your hands together in front of your chest and throw them out to the sides again. Repeat briskly 10 times.

3 With knees turned outwards, feet apart and turned out, slowly bend your knees, keeping your back straight and bottom in. When your thighs are parallel to the ground, rise slowly to upright, keeping your back straight. Repeat 5 times.

4 Kneel on all fours with your hands flat on the floor and arms straight. Slowly straighten your knees until you make a triangular shape, then gently return to your starting position. Repeat 10 times.

Run for 5-15 minutes or cycle for 10-20 minutes or weight train for 10 minutes.

Evenings

1 Skip for 3 minutes.

2 Standing with feet apart with both hands grasping your left ankle (or any point as far as you can reach without straining) try to touch your left knee with your head. Stand up straight and do the same with your right leg. Repeat 10 times.

3 Forward lunge one foot about 4 feet in front of the other, with your weight over the top of the forward knee and, resting both hands on it, bend until your thighs are parallel to the ground. Keep your other leg and your back straight. Repeat 10 times.

4 Stand straight, hands on your shoulders, elbows out, rotate twice back and twice forwards. Repeat 10 times.

Cycle for 10-20 minutes or weight train for 15 minutes or run for 5-15 minutes or 80 per cent of your maximum energy output if it is more than the time given.

Hard week three

Mornings

1 Jog slowly on the spot or around the room for 5 minutes.

2 Skip medium pace for 5 minutes.

3 Lying on your front, flat on the floor, with elbows bent and hands flat each side of your shoulders, gradually push yourself up from the floor, keeping your back and legs straight. Repeat these press-ups 10 times.

Run for 20-30 minutes or cycle for 20-25 minutes or weight train for 30 minutes or longer to your maximum energy output.

Evenings

1 Skip for 5 minutes, slowly at first, then build up to a good medium pace.

3 Standing feet apart, knees and feet turned out, bend your knees slowly, keeping a straight back until your thighs are parallel to the floor, keep your back straight while you rise slowly. Repeat 10 times.

4 Lying flat on the floor, hands behind your neck, slowly sit up, then return slowly to flat position. Repeat 10 times.

Run for 30 minutes or cycle for 50 minutes or weight train for 30 minutes, or to your maximum energy output.

Medium week four

Mornings

1 Skip slowly on the spot or around the room for 3 minutes.

2 Lying flat on the floor, raise your legs up, supporting your hips with your hands, ride a bicycle in the air for 3 minutes.

3 Five press-ups.

4 Sit on the floor and, with feet apart, hold your left ankle with both hands and try to touch your left knee with your head. Return to the sitting position and do the same with your right leg. Repeat 10 times.

5 Standing straight, twist your trunk from the waist, swinging your arms in the *same* direction, first to one side then the other. Repeat 10 times.

Run for 5-15 minutes or cycle for 10-20 minutes or weight train for 10-20 minutes. More time may be spent if this is less than 80 per cent of your optimum exertion level.

Evenings

1 Jog for 3 minutes.

2 Skip for 2 minutes.

3 Lay face down on the floor and raise yourself up on both hands, keeping them flat on the floor, either side of your shoulders. With a bounce, bring your knees forward under your chest and kick them back out straight behind you again. Repeat these squat-thrusts 5-10 times.

4 Stand straight with your feet apart and arms stretched up and outwards like the figure X. On the count of 1 bring your feet together with a jump and bring your hands together over your head, count 2, and jump your legs and arms apart in the X shape. Repeat 10 times.

Run for 10 minutes or cycle for 15 minutes or weight train for 10 minutes or 80 per cent of your total energy output.

*Based on research of Doctor Katherina Dalton.

You may have noticed that, provided that you have the use of an exercise bycicle, and a reasonable sized room with a window that can open, none of the schedule noted here need be undertaken out of doors.

This can make sense for women for a number of reasons.

If you are housebound with a young child, you can improve your general health and well being without the bind of searching out a babysitter. If you live in a 'high risk' area, you don't need to run a gauntlet of fear, or have to find a companion with whom to train. When I was in training I used to drag my two eldest girls out with me, then around 11 and 14, on my early morning and night time runs – they were the fittest youngsters on our block. (Those were the days when Richmond Ice Speed Club wouldn't allow me on to their training ice unless I was accompanied by another female, so my daughters again doubled as chaperones for the 6 a.m., Sunday ice speed sessions!).

However, the training programme I have composed, owes it workability to the present day increase of female participation in ice speed skating.

This 28 day training cycle was worked out with the assistance of young women skaters from the Streatham Ice Racing Club – their individual progress was monitored at the end of each week for three months.

I spent the first month listening to complaints and modifying some of the more frenetic exercises as a result. The second was spent in much the same way but with the added excitement of pacifying male club members who didn't see why they should be left out.

The third month proved that the cycle worked, both socially, mentally and physically, for the women, who were all at different stages of involvement with ice speed skating. They all reported feeling stronger – and they were all happy anyway. This sport has been called the toughest on earth.

It also provoked a lot of discussion on the possible merits of its use by the men and boys within the club, and eventually some of them decided to have a go at it, although there was some bewilderment over which day they should start it on . . .

CHAPTER TEN

This Sporting Life

We are all put on this earth to have a physical communication with one another and sport is a very pleasant, health-giving and fulfilling means to that end, although music, painting, mime and mathematics are the more commonly acknowledged wordless communicators.

Why are women and girls encouraged to take up all the other options, but not sport?

A ladylike pursuit?

In the General Household Survey of 1980, it was estimated that 15.5 per cent of women over the age of fifteen in England and Wales took part in various indoor sports and 24 per cent took part in outdoor sport. The corresponding figures for men are 31 per cent and 36.5 per cent respectively.

Common or garden social unacceptability of the desire for any level of achievement in physical prowess, both by and for women, is enough to keep most women and girls away from sporting precincts. Even when a dabble in the recreational context is all that's contemplated, it is often denied them.

Discrimination against women in sport isn't just the obvious dislike felt in working men's clubs, manifested by the refusal to admit women to their hallowed snooker tables. Nor is it the middle-class chauvinistic barring of women from many of the golf clubhouses, including the Royal and Ancient golf club of St Andrews, the 'home' of golf — with the added insult inherent in clubs that disallow women golfers from their courses at weekends, making access difficult for women who work during the week. It isn't the simple refusal to accept women's cricket by the Lord's cricket ground, neither is it just the patronizing attitudes and insulting banter of men guarding the entrances to sundry sports centres. More devious factors than these conspire to militate against women's participation.

The media message

The pressure on women and young girls to conform to a male-dictated social pattern is still too great.

Supposedly sexually-equal Britain is interwoven with immigrants from certain countries whose womenfolk are made to walk around covered in voluminous swathes of cloth. And this sorry state of affairs is allowed to continue by the host nation whose Bill of equality, passed in 1975, is waived for these women citizens. One wonders if the status quo is permitted out of liberalism, ignorance, apathy or design. Similarly, the media partisanship to the wagers of Holy War in Afghanistan makes no mention of the regime of purdah or the obscenities of clitoridectomy. In the name of tradition or religious freedom our society condones the oppression of women to an extent where it still affects all our lives. Just as, in the Middle East, women are offered as the reward for a successfully completed business deal, so they are still a marketable commodity here — the 'prize' implied by the advertisers for buying the right car, aftershave or aperitif. Even your popular newspaper comes complete with a 'free' woman's body, albeit made of wood pulp. Small wonder, then, that we find it so hard to break free of these masculine traditions that impede the natural right of everyone to enjoy the freedom of sporting activity.

It is another anachronism of our changing society that women and girls are still schooled towards running a home and bringing up children to the detriment of all else. This is a damaging process of acceptance which begins from the moment a girl is born.

To achieve the desired goal of attracting a male of the species, women are encouraged to rival each other in their outward appearance. Awareness of these shenanigans is gradually impressed upon the male ego in the process of his growing into adulthood. By which time if he has not been able to find for himself a proper and appropriate level at which to communicate with other human beings of the opposite gender, he will be just as bedazzled as his female counterpart by the traditional myths about himself.

The male ego has been made as precariously balanced as the female's by the insidious use of media images. These ask for a previously assumed response which will call his basic masculinity into question if he does not outwardly manifest an expected 'macho' reaction to the distorted images of women offered him. This is also so if he fails to aspire to the over-masculinized image that is thrust upon him.

The unhappy outcome of all this brainwashing is that women and girls fare very badly if they want, as they should, to control their own lives and, within that brief, their recreational and sports activities.

A tug of war

Sport, even within the framework of purely amateur recreational activity, has been used by those who govern the people to reinforce the divide and rule concept by promoting hostile competition, outward manifestations of aggression and the lauding of the killer instinct.

Within professional sport, football — not surprisingly since it has a large plebeian following helped by media propaganda — has spread these negative traits into the spectator stands, creating a similarly unruly mob to that produced by the other games held in Rome nearly 2,000 years ago.

Having produced this disgruntled and impressionable nub within a restless society, it can be used and is being used to further confuse and misdirect millions of people. (Half a million pass through football club turnstiles every Saturday.)

It is hardly surprising that the good aspects of this game are being lost and that women's football is without an audience — and also, in this cash-motivated society, without a sponsor. It is to women's credit that this game is flourishing despite all the set-backs.

It seems that, from every side, we are denied appropriate role models. At a five-a-side football tournament in the grounds of the National Sports Centre at Crystal Palace, a male coach on the sidelines was shouting: 'Mark your man' and people in the ground were calling, 'That's right, just like Kevin Keegan!' and so on. Even these interested and supportive spectators obviously hadn't heard of England players like Brenda Sempare, from Friends of Fulham LFC, or Hope Powell from Millwall Lionesses. The man who was heard to remark 'It's a pity she's not a bloke, with all that skill she could get into the men's England side', hadn't heard about Kerry Davis, the female England footballer who was signed up by an Italian side in 1985.

It is no accident that, by promoting sport as a male pastime and further 'masculinizing' the image of sport, 50 per cent of the population has been manipulated and the other 50 per cent kept quietly in their place! We will no longer be kept quietly in our place.

Money, money, money

Even more obvious than the abstract barriers created by a society founded on the unequal and uneven distribution of wealth and opportunity, are those solid obstacles produced by the male orchestrators of the international money markets.

In an economy which is becoming more and more deflated by recession, unwaged women are the most disadvantaged group. These are the women who are part of that socio-economic grouping who traditionally reject sport and recreational physical activities as inappropriate for women. However, there is a growing awareness that sport and physical recreation, when viewed as an activity that promotes health and good appearance, should be made available to them. There's the rub. With very little cash to spare for leisure-time enjoyments, together with responsibility for the supervision of their children under twelve, their participation is very difficult.

The only way to overcome the immediate dire problems of financial embarrassment and care of dependents is to provide free sports facilities, clothing and equipment, with full-time nursery provision. There would be an immediate take-up of these facilities by women.

The Women's Sports Foundation

Because of a general feeling of discontent that pervaded all stratas of women's sport, from the international competitor to the casual user of her local gym or sports centre, a group of sportswomen, most of whom had risen high through the ranks of their own sports and sports administration, got together in Spring 1984 to identify the problems and to discuss the way forward.

On 19 October 1985, the first Annual General Meeting of the Women's Sports Foundation was held at the Charteris Community Sports Centre in London. This organization brings together all women for whom sport is part of their lifestyle. Within its ever-widening network, a multitude of issues are being classified and acted upon. It is committed to improving the opportunities for women in sport at every level and its aim is to promote the interests of all women in and through sport and to gain equal opportunities and options for women. Its starting point is a positive attitude towards sportswomen. It recognizes that recreational and fitness activities like aerobics, jogging and weights are becoming an important part of the lifestyle of many women and, at the same time is aware that in top-level competitive sport, British women win more medals than British men. It provides a supportive system of sub-groups within its regionalization programme and these groups will ensure that all the problems facing women and girls in sports and associated physical activities are addressed and, given the limitations of our social system, overcome.

'Daft!'

Illustrations of discrimination in support of the need for a women-only umbrella organization are countless. The Golfing Union of Ireland added a clause to their constitution which states that any club which allows women full voting rights in their club shall be disqualified from the Union, in the wake of an attempt by one golf club to allow women full membership.

A Leeds newspaper published a piece after a decision by the Leisure Services Department to make certain times at the City's Sports centres all-women activity centres with crèches which was headlined: 'Daft! All-women sports plan.' This contained trivializing quotes from the deputy manager, and a quote from 'thrice married Mr Glen Lowe of Gipton, Leeds, an ex-miner', who said 'Women should be kept behind the kitchen sink and then allowed up to the bedroom in the evening.'

Another 'quality' newspaper carried the headline: 'Women must be ready to break fingernails.' This was a comment by the National Coaching Director for British Athletics, Mr Frank Dick.

One of the first editions of the more popular style *Today* newspaper sub-headed a women's sports item: 'Girls will be girls when it comes to football' and continued its patronizing way into 'they were late for their Sunday training and there were no changing rooms — just quick flashes of knickers in the backs of their cars. They didn't even have enough balls, and they'd swapped their shirts with a French team.'

The *Daily Mail,* as an example of the middle-of-the-road Press, sponsored the 'Cresta Run Challenge'. They announced that they were searching for a champion, a young *man* full of courage, spirit and judgement, someone of superb physical condition with super-quick reflexes, who responds to a sporting challenge. This challenge was run in conjunction with the St Moritz tobogganing club who administer the men-only Cresta run. The run was established in 1887 and women raced until 1929, but it was decided at that time that it had particular dangers for women because of the stress put on their bodies during the high-speed event! This piece of pseudo-medical mumbo jumbo has never been rejected by them since.

The British Broadcasting Corporation transmitted a ninety-five minute programme review of sport for 1985. Three minutes forty-nine seconds were devoted to women's sport. After reading a critique by the Chair of the Women's Sports Foundation, Celia Brackenridge, in *Sportswoman* magazine, the BBC Assistant Head of Sport wrote to the WSF: 'We do not intend to cover any sports because they are specifically male or female if they do not measure up in our judgement to the standard that we believe should be exposed on our screens.' The WSF asks: 'Whose screens, Mr Anderson?'

Towards 2001

When the boxer Barry McGuigan complained publicly about his opponent's comments, 'He keeps saying I'm a woman and I don't like it', he typified the attitude of many an unthinking male. I know a few women who, were it not for their female qualities and devotion to non-violence, would have laid him out.

There are many sportsmen whose fear of being beaten by a woman borders on the paranoid. With the gap in performance narrowing, gradually at top level, but more quickly at recreational and club participatory level, sportsmen are going to have to live with the looming equality of sportswomen.

At the same time, women should abjure attempts to compare them with men, whether this be done in a favourable manner or insultingly.

That women have a different bodily structure and biological purpose to that of the male is self-evident. That this precludes women from taking part in and enjoying sports and physical recreation is a nonsense.

Women have physical abilities far superior to those of men. After all — without us, men would not be born. Scientists, in recognition of that very real weak link in the male power structure, are attempting to redress the balance by engineering the growth of embryos to term in women (for the present time) without a womb. This gives a whole new meaning to biological warfare.

We live in a society that condones 'manly' attributes in men as self-confident competitiveness with a desire for self-fulfillment, and condemns these same attributes in women — especially in sport, which is still viewed as a male preserve.

One of the most prevalent underlying reasons for the reluctance to support the image of strong women is that, at the present time, strong women are often those whose lives do not revolve around the needs and dictates of men — lesbians.

However, the women's liberation movement has its fair share of heterosexual women, and this will grow as the equality of women increases.

Homosexuality in itself does not necessarily politicize its bearer. There are probably more lesbian women in the armed forces and in other uniformed services than there are sitting outside or sympathizing with the protestors at Greenham Common airbase. Sport is of a similar pattern. That there are many lesbians in sport is a fact, that some are top-flight competitors is true and that some just like an occasional game of badminton is also true. That lesbian women are a threat to heterosexual women is untrue. Heterosexism is as rampant in sport as the sexism from which we suffer. It is all the more painful when it makes its presence felt in all-women environments where we should all feel safe and secure.

The women who will watch two men wrestling together or otherwise knocking each other about with impunity are the same women who complained to a female sports centre supervisor that two women were cuddling and kissing each other in the showers, and what was the supervisor going to do about it. This little anecdote was told by the supervisor at a meeting of a new women's organization called Lesbians In Sport (See page 123).

Women's sport and recreational activities bring together all women in a common enjoyment, in much the same ways as the ancient craft guilds brought a pooling of skills and social and business contact to men in the middle ages.

The Women's Sports Foundation will provide this contact for all women, but it will also behave as a more highly evolved union.

At least the powers that be cannot transport us or hang us for insurrection. Neither can they apply the 'lock out', as our union was formed because of an already operating lock out!

I remember having to wait outside my club's changing room door, while the committee used the room to discuss the pros and cons of my application to join. After what seemed like an eternity, I was ushered in and told that one of the major concerns was that if I was made a full member, I would become eligible for the committee; the air of the committee was often decidedly blue and therefore unsuitable for a lady.

Wondering what polite defence I could make, I asked if that meant that none of us were allowed to swear on the ice any more, and they allowed me to join but only as a junior (under sixteen, with no voting rights on the committee). I was twenty-nine years of age.

Some years later, I invoked the new Sex Equality Bill, earned the right to pay full subs — and those early fears were realized when I was elected to serve on the committee.

I have just completed ten years of service as the Streatham Ice Racing Club's Secretary and I was rewarded with election to the Chair in 1986.

Back in 1977, I retired from competition, started coaching and became the first female judge of ice speed skating. Last year I became the first woman to qualify as a full referee, sitting on the referees' panel.

I have had the pleasure of seeing, not only little skaters, including my six children, grow taller than me, but also the participation of women increasing in my own sport, once considered to be for men only.

My granddaughter, Michelle, will be twenty-one in the year 2001 and will spend her sportswomanhood in the twenty-first century. She enjoys karate, netball, dance, BMX racing and wants to be a speed skater. I shall leave the last words on women's sport to her — the words she spoke to me as she got on the ice at my home rink for the first time: 'I think it's brilliant — watch me!'

Useful Addresses

WSF
Women's Sports Foundation, 'Parkholme',
Collegiate Crescent,
Sheffield, S10

WSF
South London Women's Centre,
Wesley House,
4 Wild Court,
London, WC2B 5AU

AENA
All England Netball Association, Francis House,
Francis Street,
London, SW1P 1DE

AEWHA
All England Women's Hockey
Association,
Argyle House,
29-31 Euston Road,
London, NW1

AEWLA
All England Women's Lacrosse
Association,
Secretary,
Ms J. Cantell,
16 Upper Woburn Place,
London, WC1H 0QJ

BHS
British Horse Society,
British Equestrian Centre,
Stoneleigh,
Kenilworth,
Warwickshire, CV8 2LR

British Korfball Association
2 Torrington Close,
Mereworth,
Maidstone,
Kent

BSAD
British Sports Association for
the Disabled,
Dr RJ Price,
Director and Chief Executive,
Hayward House,
Barnard Crescent,
Aylesbury,
Buckinghamshire, HP21 8PP

Campaign for Press and Broadcasting Freedom Women's Group
9 Poland Street,
London, W1V 3DG

EOWA
English Olympic Wrestling Association,
H.I. Jacob O.B.E.
2 Huxley Drive,
Bramhall,
Stockport,
Cheshire

Equal Opportunities Commission
Overseas House,
Quay Street,
Manchester, M3 3HN

Ladies Amateur Fencing Union
42 Grove Cresent,
Kingston Upon Thames,
Surrey

LIS
Lesbians In Sport,
c/o London Lesbian and Gay Centre,
69 Cowcross Street,
London,EC1

NSA
National Skating Association of
Great Britain,
15-27 Gee Street,
London, EC1V 3RE

The Sports Council,
16 Upper Woburn Place,
London, WC1H 0QP

WCA
Women's Cricket Association,
Administrative Officer,
Ms C. Duley,
16 Upper Woburn Place,
London, WC1H 0QF

WFA
Women's Football Association,
Secretary,
Linda Whitehead,
11 Portsea Mews,
Portsea Place,
London, W2 2BN

WLBSA
World Ladies Billiards &
Snooker Association,
Secretary, Mandy Fisher,
Brandy Lodge,
Lebanon Drive,
Walsoken,
Wisbech,
Cambridgeshire, PE13 5RX
or
Gaye Jones,
Tournament Director,
33 Fernhurst Road,
Ashford,
Middlesex, TW15 1AQ

Women's Professional Golf Association
Apollo House,
The Belfry,
Wishaw,
Sutton Coldfield,
W. Midlands, B76 9PT

Women's Squash Rackets Association
354 Upper Richmond Road West,
Sheen,
London, SW14 8QN

Australia

Council for Health, Physical Educatiion and Recreation
P.O. Box 1,
Kingswood,
South Australia 5062

Department of Youth, Sport and Recreation
570 Bourke Street,
Melbourne 3000

Bulgaria

International Federation of Sports Acrobatics
Boul 'Tolboukhine' 18,
1000 SOFIA

Canada

CAAWS
Canadian Association for the Advancement of Women and Sport/
Association Canadienne Pour l'Advancement de la Femme et la Sport.
PO Box 3769
Station C
Ottawa
Ontario K1Y 4JB

Canadian Amateur (Ice) Hockey Association
333 River Road
Vanier
Ontario K1L 8H9

Ontario Women's (Ice) Hockey Association
4206 Greybrook Crescent
Mississagua
Ontario L4W 3G6

China

All-China Sports Federation
9 Tiyuguan Road
Peking
People's Republich of China

Japan

Women's Sports Foundation
Sports 21
Enterprise Ltd
3-36-23-202
Nishara
Shibuya-ku
Tokyo

USA

WSF
Women's Sports Foundation
195 Moulton Street
San Francisco
CA 94123
or
342 Madison Avenue
Suite 728
New York
NY 10017

TF
Triathlon Federation
Lookout Road
Tuxedo Park
New York
NY 10987

AL
Anti-defamation League
B'nai B'rith
823 United Nations Plaza
New York
NY 10017
(Anti-racist sports posters, such as Tiffany Chin, Evelyn Ashford, Debbie Armstrong with the legend 'If you really believe in America, prejudice is foul play', available from this organisation)

Index